MY LIFE
MY LEADERS
MY LORD

THE WISDOM OF A COUNTRY BOY

DR. LOUIS B. LYNN

- - - - - - - - - - - -

DEDICATION

To My Parents

My parents, Lawton and Dorothy Lynn, raised me and my two sisters to focus on getting our education, applying our education, and sharing our education. They accomplished this goal while starting their own farm and eventually launching a business after years of sharecropping. While they accomplished their fiscal goals, they concentrated on shaping my character and aligning my worldview with Godly, spirit-led beliefs.

To My Wife

Audrey Johnson and I grew up in the same neighborhood. She was my childhood sweetheart and my first date. Like my parents, we passed on the education mantra to our children that my parents applied to me and my siblings. As our elders did, Audrey and I have lived our lives and raised our children under Godly, spirit-led beliefs. During the writing of this book, Audrey encouraged me and stood by me just as she did during my journey to obtain my doctorate, my career journey, and my business journey.

ACKNOWLEDGEMENTS

I offer a character and faith disclaimer up front. If I've penned anything that offends anyone or is politically incorrect or just plain stupid, please charge it to my HEAD and not to my HEART.

To my wife of 50+ years, Audrey, who provided encouragement and support during the writing of this book. My writing began about the time that Audrey was diagnosed with cancer. While going through chemotherapy and radiation treatments, including several short hospital stays, she continued to encourage me to finish writing the book. We had t-shirts printed with "God's Got This" on the front and "Put me in Coach" on the back. We gave these T-shorts to other cancer patients as well as others facing life challenges to include marital, financial, spiritual, career and other health issues.

To my children, Adrienne, Krystal, and Bryan, who are a gift from God to us. They were obedient to our parenting, which they recognized was similar to the way their grandparents had raised us. They are good children who never got into trouble during their teen days. We are extremely blessed with our grandchildren, for they show love and respect to Audrey and me. My children and my children's children all accept and embrace the family mantra that "education is the tide that lifts all boats."

To my sisters, who lived "the journey" with me during our childhood and teen days. My sisters encouraged me in education, in marriage, in business, and in my seminary-spiritual journey. They are great sisters-in-law to my wife and great aunts to my children. I thank my sisters for keeping family records used to verify the accuracy and details of the "journey stories" presented in this book. Mom and Dad are surely smiling down from heaven on the adults we've become.

To theologian and author deTreville F. Bowers, Jr. (Det), who is accomplished in several professions. He is respected and recognized as a preacher, a businessman, and a lawyer. Over the years, he has owned and started several businesses. He also has a track record as a timber enthusiast. Pastor Bowers devoted most of his career to Christian ministry as pastor of Christ Church of the Carolinas in Columbia. When I met Det, he was senior pastor of a progressive nondenominational church in town. So, in addition to attending morning services at my church, I attended afternoon services at Pastor Bowers' church. I have 50 plus CD recordings of Pastor Bowers' sermons delivered in an expository style. It was his pastoral style and his personal interactions with me that encouraged me to sign up for the Marketplace Ministry program at his alma mater, Columbia International University. Pastor Bowers authored several religious books, including a 52-week devotional study titled *Godspeed*. I have referenced several of the weekly journeys from Pastor Bowers' devotional in this book. When I shared my plans to author this book, he personally gave me permission to employ materials from his writing without assigning honor to the author, as printed on the USBN page. The written and spoken words of Pastor Bowers have had significant influence on the writing of My Life and My Leaders as integrated into my relations with My Lord.

To the pastors whose preaching and teaching I sat under, as well as whose advising and counseling impacted my life. And to the professors and advisors at Columbia International University who I took courses from during my studies for Marketplace Ministry.

And finally, I acknowledge and give praise to my Lord, Jesus the Christ. I pray that this book gives honor and glory to the Lord. I also pray that this book answers my daily petition, "Out of my life let Jesus shine," and that it helps make ready a people prepared for the Lord!

ENDORSEMENTS

COUNTRY BOY WISDOM

As you read *The Wisdom of a Country Boy*, you will be inspired by the author's example for each of us as we search to find our best selves. Dr. Lynn has been my Clemson University classmate, my encouragement for over 50 years, and my guide as a long-serving member of Clemson's Board of Trustees. This is a wonderful story of faith, positive outlook, and dedication.

Dr. James F. Barker
President Emeritus, Clemson University

Inspiring, motivating, insightful, and a must-read in today's challenges of professional and personal uncertainty. This author, whom I deem as an iconic mentor and leader, challenges us to laugh at our adversities, cry with joy when blessings are revealed, and embrace wisdom as a beacon of light for others to do the same.

Cassius F. Butts
*Former 2x Presidential Appointee,
Speaker & Author*

In the few short years that I have gotten to know my friend Dr. Louis Lynn, it is abundantly clear that he is a uniquely gifted individual. I have come to know him to have a tender heart, a brilliant mind, and a strong faith in God. His life is proof that modeling integrity, faithfulness, and kindness will open many doors in life. But his wisdom and work ethic have helped him to excel beyond what most people could imagine possible.

Pastor Brian Boyles
Church on Main

At this critical juncture in developing the next generation of agricultural leaders, Dr. Lynn's life story offers "the wisdom of a country boy" in a prolific writing that gives hope to aspiring leaders in the field of agriculture. He is profoundly open about life's uncertainties, yet unequivocally confident in his faith and God's plan and purpose for his life. Dr. Lynn, in facing life's adversities, lives his belief, *"And we know that all things work together for the good to them that love God, to them who are the called according to his purpose."* (Romans 8:28).

Dr. Saundra Glover
USDA

The Wisdom of a Country Boy is too modest a descriptor for Dr. Lynn's roaring ambition, overwhelming generosity, keen wit, and unshakable faith. As a member of our Board of Trustees, he has guided the National Urban League through unprecedented challenges while embodying our mission of empowering communities and changing lives. His story is the making of an exemplary American whom I am proud to call a mentor and a friend.

Marc H. Morial
President and CEO
National Urban League

A blueprint for achieving success that should be a must-read for up-and-coming youth and a heartfelt reminder to those who overcame similar odds. A must-read for everyone.

Diane Sumpter
Director
SC Minority Business Development Center

As a highly respected mentor and friend for many years, Dr. Louis Lynn has shared with me countless points of personal and professional wisdom fostered by many of his life's lessons. I have always believed so many others could benefit from his teachings, and it is exciting to see that opportunity manifested with this timely platform. To allow others a glimpse into his fascinating journey is a rich and prolific gift.

Dontá L. Wilson
Chief Consumer & Small Business Banking Officer
Truist Financial Corporation

TABLE OF CONTENTS

INTRODUCTION

My name is Dr. Louis Lynn. On the pages that follow, I have presented reflections of some of the most memorable events that have occurred on my journey so far since my birth in 1949. What you will discover first and foremost is that the Bible has been foundational in shaping my life. From years of studying the Bible, I have found that there is a central thread throughout the scriptures of mankind being on a journey. It reveals that each of us are on a personal journey on the road of life. The Bible tells us stories of real-life men and women whose journey through life portrays the love God has for His creation. It also reveals the character of God. God has given man free will to govern his life. God did not want mindless men to follow His plan without thought.

He wanted men to choose to become a part of the family of God and live under His will for their life. In my opinion, the journey is made easier if we allow God to direct our steps. This belief stems from the teachings of my parents, who emphatically believed the Bible and that God was willing and able to help them on their journey. Of all the things my parents taught me, the most important was to love God and respect His Word.

I belong to the Baby Boomer generation, who were afforded a unique set of opportunities that enabled many of us to become world changers, at least in our part of the world. We had greater access to educational opportunities, a view of the world from our living room, and the benefit of federal laws that gave previously denied access to jobs and careers for minorities. My own journey was shaped by my family and my community, who spoon-fed me wisdom through old sayings, proverbs, and idioms passed down to them from past generations in the African American community. These Southern, colloquial sayings became foundational to molding my belief systems and character development. For they not only helped to form my personal life, but they influenced my spiritual, civic, and business life as well. I don't believe I would have become the man I am today had these sayings not helped guide me throughout my journey.

The faith that began in my home and that was strengthened by the various leaders I met throughout my childhood, my educational journey, and into my adulthood gave me wisdom to navigate my career, my marriage, and my financial status, and even now they aide me as I contemplate what retirement will look like. I have not lived in a vacuum, and due to the media-explosion that transcended throughout my life, I have also been influenced by secular writers who also saw life as a journey. Hence, I have also referenced words of wisdom from prominent secular figures who have inspired me. In the three segments of this book, My Life, My Leaders, and My Lord, I hope you too will find encouragement that will enhance your journey, blessing your life as mine has been blessed.

SECTION 1

MY LIFE

CHAPTER 1

MY STORY – MY JOURNEY

History and Legacy

I am an African American man who proudly embraces my heritage, and I have committed myself to following my God-given destiny. My elders descended from former Africans who were taken from their native land and brought to this nation as slaves. Later they were emancipated. However, while enslaved, much of their culture was changed to create in them a new person, no longer African but not American either. There were name changes and tribal rituals lost through the years of enslavement. What they believed about God also changed. The slaves were first preached a form of Christianity as indoctrination. Over time, more slaves were exposed to the Word of God and heard of the promises of God inherent in the Bible. They soon saw God as a loving Father who wanted their children to have a good life. As former slaves and now freedmen became literate, they were able to read the Bible for themselves. They also embraced the concept of life being a journey, with the final destination being heaven. The Bible combined with African proverbs that were handed down through the generations encouraged them to believe that in order to see where we are going, we not only must *remember* where we have been, but we must *understand* where we have been and how we got there. This view of life was passed down to their children.

My parents belonged to what is known as the Silent Generation, yet they were anything but silent in our home. For as long as I can remember, they were constantly teaching me in the tradition of their elders through proverbs, wise sayings, and just plain common sense. They believed in my potential, yet they knew that for a young African American man potential was not enough. They knew that in order for me to be able to fully reach my potential, I needed to have a strong character and integrity. They knew that without moral values, all the knowledge in the world would not help me. They exposed me to a community that shared their values and beliefs. In addition, they gave me room to dream and opportunity to go after my dreams. Unfortunately, many children today are not growing up in this type of environment, and they have become frustrated concerning their future. Even though they may have the education, they sometimes lack the country boy wisdom to make their dreams come true.

Growing up, I heard so many words that stuck with me, giving me an appreciation of "words that speak to the sentiments I am feeling." When I hear a phrase or a saying I like, I write it down and save those words for future reference. This has given me a huge repertoire from which to draw, and many of my favorite sayings will be included in this book. The most enduring words I have shared were passed down to me by my elders. They were centered around truths like that found in Proverbs 29:18, "*Where there is no vision, the people perish.*"

In my adult years, I came to understand the importance of chronicling your story. Along with my teachers and community leaders, prominent personalities who had achieved a degree of notoriety also inspired me. For example, there were two celebrities that addressed the importance of chronicling your own story. The celebrated African American poet Maya Angelou wrote, "There is no greater agony than bearing an untold story inside you."[1] These words encouraged me to put my pen to paper. Also, the words of renowned actress Cicely Tyson, "Knowing your generational story firms the ground upon which you stand. It makes your life, your struggles, and triumphs bigger than your lone existence. It connects you to a grand plotline."[2] These expressions spoke a message to my heart that I could understand.

My personal philosophy was solidified when I read Pastor Rick Warren's book, *The Purpose Driven Life,*[3] which helped me understand that each of us has a purpose and our quest is to find that purpose and fulfill it. Prolific thinkers like these notable figures helped me to recognize that I needed to pray and seek God to reach for my destiny, live it out, and then to chronicle it for future generations. I saw my life to be an unveiling of "who I am" and "Whose I am." Not only was I an African American, but I was shaped by my Creator, God, who knew what my purpose in this world was to be. This same God wanted to be involved in helping develop that purpose at every stage of my life. I consider myself fortunate to have come into a relationship with God at an early age. I believe that it was the Hand of God leading and guiding me through early life experiences that opened doors where my dreams would be fulfilled. Most importantly, I learned that the Bible has timeless truths that when applied help us reach our goals.

Choosing to follow that instruction of course is up to us. However, if we do choose to follow it, our journey is more fruitful on this side of heaven, and it continues through to the next life with even greater benefits than we could imagine. According to pollsters today, the majority of people in our society look at life as just things happening by coincidence. As a believer in Christ Jesus, I don't believe in coincidences. I think that when we give God our lives, the road we travel is one that God directs, and on that road, we find GOD-incidences! If we lean into those God-incidences, they will bless our life.

> **"Our character is a journey, not a destination."**

As I look back on the way I raised my own children, I found myself often repeating the words of my parents. For the words that they spoke to me were like me walking in wet cement; everywhere they fell, they left an impression. The older I got, the more I appreciated the wise words my parents and grandparents shared with me, even when they were not intentional. An old proverb states that "our character is a journey, not a destination."[4] Through my elders, I gained a great deal of wise advice about how to live this life to make it count for something. Some of my most memorable tidbits of advice include:

- Our character is what we do when no one is looking.[5]

- Character is made by what you stand for, and your reputation is made by what you fall for.[6]

- Your character is who you are, and your reputation is who people think you are.[7]

- Worry about your character, not your reputation.[8]

- Let your character speak louder than your words.[9]

- It's not how we make mistakes; it's how we correct them.[10]

These words and many more like them shaped my character development and remain that "still small voice" in my ear steering me into making good decisions, pushing me to take risks into unknown territories, and always guiding me through challenging situations.

I believe that the best classroom for our youth is sitting at the feet of an elderly person. When an elder dies, it is as if a library burns. The treasury of their experience and knowledge is lost to the world. Over the years, I also learned that another word aligned with character is courage. Adversity doesn't develop character as much as it reveals character. The achievement of goals that contributed to my successes in life have always been more rewarding when I was pushed beyond my comfort zone. The benefits of moving beyond established limits were something that I witnessed every day of my life.

Watching my family, I saw the hardship of struggles and the joys of successes. My father didn't just tell me how to live; he lived his everyday life and let me watch him do it. He also was a Dad who applied the principles of encouragement for his children to do the right thing with a few pats on the back. I contend that developing character in children can be enhanced by pats on the back if applied low enough, hard enough, and often enough. The discipline I received as a child did not make me resentful of my father. As early as pre-school, when I thought about what I wanted to be when I grew up, it was clear to me; I wanted to be like my Dad.

Looking back at the love and guidance my parents and grandparents poured into me during my developmental years, I know they were looking ahead to my life as an adult. My folks and others like them recognized that coddling parents often handicap their children by making their lives too easy. Instead, my parents believed that good child-rearing was keeping your children's feet on the ground and putting some responsibility on their shoulders. They were wise enough to know, as Frederick Douglas said in his dialogues to slave owners in 1855, "It is easier to build strong children than it is to repair broken adults."

Family Must Look Out for Family
Family is the ultimate source of strength and resilience.
Together, they can overcome any obstacle and achieve greatness.

One of the families I grew up watching on television was the Waltons. Another favorite of mine was the Jeffersons. While you could argue that both TV shows were programmed for a different generation than the current one, the child-rearing principles exhibited in these shows are timeless. My home could best be described as a blend of "old school" teaching with a vision for a better future that my parents believed would come. When you grow up in a family that has entrenched certain values and principles into their daily living, then you just do what is presented to you, without question. As I grew older, I noticed that the bond that linked "family" was not only bloodline. In my blood family, there was no doubt that we shared a love for one another. However, family also included those who shared your good, bad, and ugly moments and still loved you, even if they weren't blood kin. The feelings we shared also included the respect and joy that we received from one another. I have concluded that family bonding is easy if you treat your family like friends and your friends like family. A guiding principle for parenting in my family has always been based on scripture: "*Train up a child in the way he should go: And when he is old, he will not depart from it*" (Proverb 22:6). Another scripture they held to was: "*Behold, children are a gift of the Lord, the fruit of the womb is a reward*" (Psalm 127:3). Training steeped in love, shaped with recognition of the value of each family member, including the children, describes the happy home I grew up in.

There is an old saying, "You can choose your friends, but you can't choose your relatives." South African Bishop and theologian Desmond Tutu said that "You don't choose your family. They are God's gift to you, as you are to them." Fortunately, I was blessed to have a number of first cousins who were raised in the same kind of home, with the same kind of work ethic as well as social, civic, and spiritual beliefs that I was raised with. My parents and my cousins' parents (my uncles and aunts) coordinated events that allowed our families to participate in and enjoy mutual family activities. Our relationship could be described as cousin/sibling relationships. These sibling family events included Sunday dinners, church events, neighborhood social events, sports events, and school events. A benefit of our activities was that I got to know my cousins very well. I was the oldest male cousin on both sides of the family, so I had the privilege of getting to know all of my cousins as we grew up. Grandpa Lynn, Uncle Neal, and my Dad attended the family's ancestral church, which also gave me and my sisters even more opportunities to interact with some of our cousins.

My Dad and one of his brothers (O'Neal) both had retail stores. As a result of their similar businesses, I spent a lot of time playing with and working with Uncle Neal's kids. Since Uncle Neal lived in town, his kids often provided day labor on my Dad's farm, helping with tobacco harvest or working as helpers in the butcher shop. Uncle Neal, Aunt Bert, and my parents have all gone home to be with the Lord. Yet the memories of all the good times we had will always be with me. I remember fondly my Dad and Mom's other siblings, who included Edith, James, Robert, Louie, Benjamin, Joy, Harden, Louie B, Vasthi, O'Neal, Marvin, and Ruth. All these immediate family members along with their spouses lovingly poured into my life through words of wisdom, words and actions emphasizing proper discipline, celebrating life's milestones (graduations, marriage, career); plus, they shared moments of joy, and sadness when sorrowful seasons of life occurred. Life lessons from my Uncles and Aunts further influenced my view of what family looked like. Their contributions were some of the building blocks that have added real value to my life.

As adult cousins, we still maintain social, spiritual, and civic family relationships. Unfortunately, due to career mobility moves and families settling in states separated by hundreds of miles, our family relationships with cousins are not as robust as they were during our childhood days. The children of my cousins and my children have not enjoyed the same type and level of family ties that I enjoyed. Even so, childhood memories during individual visits with cousins or at family reunions are heartwarming reminders of the GOOD OLD DAYS. Even being miles apart, nothing has broken our family's bond and love for each other. I am blessed to have family, friends, and God in my life.

My Life at Home Was Safe, But Outside Threats Were Not Safe

I was born in 1949, and as a boy growing up, my parents taught me the way things were done in the rural South where we lived. They were the first ones that taught me what it meant to live under Jim Crow. Their lives had been governed by Jim Crow legislation, where racial segregation was maintained throughout the South by establishing separate public facilities like schools and libraries and even public transportation, restrooms, and water fountains; and by enacting laws, they also regulated voting practices, employment policies, and social practices for Whites and Jim Crow (a negative slur used for African Americans).

When we went to town, we were told that we had to drink from Colored water fountains. We had to purchase sandwiches and meals from the back window of White restaurants. There was never a time that you could sit down in those restaurants; fortunately, however, there were also some Black restaurants. Both my grandfathers and my father experienced racism firsthand. They witnessed the cruel and often fatal deeds of the Ku Klux

Klan (KKK). Those deeds included KKK parades in small towns and cross burnings in the fields. As a child, I remember several occasions when our family was traveling back home in the evening when my Dad saw KKK cross-burning incidents. He always told us kids to get down on the floor of the car as he slowly drove by. Those occurrences left images of fear and conflict within me that began to fade as racial harmony improved during my young adult days. In fact, it was during my teen years that I saw attitudes and behaviors change for the better in response to the efforts of the Civil Rights Movement. I knew that more work needed to be done, but I believed the words of the Civil Rights Anthem—"We Shall Overcome."[11] Memories of hearing this song ringing out on the airwaves and at churches and other public events instilled a sense of pride in me for who I was and for the community I was a part of.

As a child growing up in the sixties, however, it could not be denied that daily television reports showed a part of the South that even my parents were not acquainted with. I saw water hoses driving peaceful marchers off the streets with torrents of water. I saw Black men and women spit on at lunch counters. I saw hatred spewed out of people such as I had never witnessed before. There were stories of people losing their lives as they protested unfair laws like those prohibiting their right to vote. It seemed as if every day there was abuse toward those Blacks trying to gain integration into public schools and/or attain equal employment. For many people in my age group, it took years, even into our adulthood, for those images to not stir up emotion. Attending Clemson and being around people who desired racial harmony helped to eradicate bad memories. Yet, even as an old man, media reports on those days can still trigger sad memories.

LIFE IS NOT TIED WITH WRAPPING AND A BOW ... BUT IT IS STILL A GIFT!

Life is God's gift to us.
What we do with it is our gift to God.[12]

"A penny saved is a penny earned"[13] is a saying that has been around in this country a long time. As strange as it seems, at one time in this country saving part of your income was not only encouraged but was an integral part of a family's plan. In fact, in my community many Black churches would urge their members to give ten percent to the Lord and ten percent to yourself, and then live off the other 80 percent of your salary. The root of this practice came from expressions like this one that is often attributed to Benjamin Franklin. It certainly helped to shape the way I viewed money.

I recognized early in life that saving part of your earnings builds capital, capital that can give you an advantage when opportunities arise. This kind of understanding can be classified as wisdom, and that kind of wisdom is not necessarily learned from a book. This familiar expression about a penny can afford us opportunity to compare our life to a coin. Each of us has 24 hours a day to spend any way you wish, but you can only spend them once. A friend told me that sometimes when responding to their parents they'd roll their eyes and say, "Dad! Life is hard." The response he received from his Dad was, "Wear a helmet."

I attained a great deal of this kind of wisdom while I was working alongside my Daddy and my grandfathers. They taught me how to be successful in life, with simple country wisdom. Now, at this stage of my life, I am still learning from their words of wisdom. I celebrate those times when someone gives me sound advice and all I can say is, "Yes, Lord!" It happens also when I give sage advice or counsel to someone else. Even with my repertoire of stored-up wise sayings, I take in teaching and learning things with humility because I believe in the saying, "If you are filled with pride, then you will have no room for wisdom."[14]

"If you are filled with pride, then you will have no room for wisdom."

One of my earliest memories of growing up and working in the rich farm fields of South Carolina is that of my elders giving me advice and counsel through one-line Southern expressions. Their old-timey expressions made obvious points that were self-explanatory. Many of the things they said followed in the tradition of their elders who had passed down their wisdom through the same kinds of expressions. The things they said not only got my attention but also got into my heart. They instilled in me a sense of what was right and what was wrong. Even more than that, they gave me the keys to living a good and successful life. Motivational speaker and business strategist Tony Robbins emphasizes in his coaching and self-help seminars that, "Life is a gift, and it offers us the privilege, opportunity, and responsibility to give something back by becoming more."[15] My parents' and grandparents' encouragement always made me want to become better. African proverbs and Southern one-liners were the truths they used to form my foundation.

Seeing these truths modeled in the daily living of my parents and grandparents reinforced the importance of the expressions that they spoke. Along with the education I received from the schools I attended, these became the companion building blocks of my knowledge and character-building. These wise sayings from family, teachers, preachers, and the many other influential people in my community are the cornerstones of my educational journey, my career journey, and my life's journey. At this stage of life, I know that the greatest gift you can receive is another day of life, lived with wisdom. In my daily prayers I often say, "Thank you, Lord, for waking me up this morning and starting me on my way." Then, I have the assurance that as I am on my way, wisdom will direct me into making good decisions.

CHAPTER 2

MY EARLIEST CHILDHOOD MEMORIES

"Right Actions Only Flow from Right Hearts" (Proverbs 4:23)

Daddy was the role model and chief executive of the "living right model" that he and Mom expected from our family. I can never leave out the impact that my praying mother invested in my early childhood development. She was a woman of faith and prayer. Mom was also firm but fair as she raised me. I laugh at the Momma sayings, like "Boy, you are smelling yourself" when she wanted to throttle or check my arrogant or disrespectful attitudes. Or when she said, "Boy, go sit down somewhere" when my behavior was borderline inappropriate or when she was tired of my mischievous antics. It was constantly hearing things like these that shaped my character as a child and became foundational in my adult life as a parent and as a businessman.

As I witnessed her prayers being answered, it became living proof of the reality of God. As I began to pray and see results, I discovered that God loved me, and He wanted me to know that I could count on Him to be there for me. As a young boy growing up, I also was spoon-fed the teaching that I am the only one who I had to impress and that I am the only one in charge of my attitude and happiness. Stating things like "A bad attitude is like a flat tire. You can't go anywhere until you change it", helped to reinforce a positive attitude in my life, which has benefited me greatly throughout my life. It was during my childhood that I learned that even if you cannot change the people around you, you can change the people that you choose to be around. I also had my parents prove to me over and over that "No" is a complete sentence.

> **"A bad attitude is like a flat tire. You can't go anywhere until you change it"**

During my childhood days, my family would have been considered to be a Black middle-class family because of the things they had accumulated and the respect that they earned as a result of their entrepreneurialism. In current times, we would be considered as poor, but as a child I never felt that way. My parents and grandparents were proud people who didn't complain, for they appreciated the blessings that the LORD had bestowed upon them. I don't remember ever missing a meal. I especially remember that my Grandpa used to say before meals, "Boy, get all that you want, but want all that you get." When I overestimated my appetite with a stacked plate, he would make me sit at the table until I had eaten all that I had put on my plate.

> **"Boy, get all that you want, but want all that you get."**

Grandpa's life lesson has been with me since childhood. And as an adult, I incorporated Grandpa's life lesson in how I manage and utilize GOD-GIVEN resources in civic and social settings, in my family life, and in how I run my business. Even my management style reflects Grandpa's life lessons, when I advise or observe when someone has "more on their plate than they can handle." As I look at the world around me now and see so many people who are depressed and have a negative view of life, I recognize more and more that the instruction I had growing up was more valuable than gold. As a matter of fact, in recent times, when I share some of these "country boy sayings," young folks apply current day slang and say that they are enjoying the gems that I'm dropping on them.

> **"I incorporated Grandpa's life lesson in how I manage and utilize GOD-GIVEN resources in civic and social settings, in my family life, and in how I run my business."**

CHAPTER 3

My K-12 Education
Kindergarten and Second Grade

One child, one teacher, one book, one pen can change the world.[16]

In my early years, the schools in the South were segregated. However, as I was growing up, Black and White families living in the same neighborhood normally did not object to little Black boys and little White boys playing together. We would play street basketball, football, and baseball. We also worked together as hired hands on farms to get the crops harvested on time. However, because of segregated schools, when we mingled with the larger community, we maintained separate groups of friends with no social integration.

When I started kindergarten, my parents were just ending their sharecropping agreement and starting out on their newly purchased farm. Since my grandfather had a "Mom and Pop" grocery store in town, my parents let me stay in town with my grandparents Monday through Friday so they could help watch me and so that I could attend school. My parents did not live in the public school district where my grandparents lived, so I attended kindergarten at a private Catholic school whose mission was to serve the Black community. However, every weekend, I went to be with my parents and sister at our home on the farm.

I had the privilege of attending school in Hartsville, South Carolina, for my first three years. St. Joseph Catholic School began as a missionary parish to serve the Hartsville African American community. Established in 1945, the parish operated a school and convent in addition to a church. By 1953, the school, which only served K-7 African American students, had an enrollment of approximately 90 students. Spending my early formative years at St. Joseph Catholic has served me well through my lifetime. My spiritual training from kindergarten to second grade reflected the same values that I was taught at home. It emphasized what I heard on Sundays at church. This meant that my spiritual training was in the same vein throughout the week. Fortunately for me, those same values also existed throughout our community and have continued to do so over the years. Generations since then have continued holding fast to those same values. In fact, that historical school and church closed in 1967; however, that school building is now a historic landmark thanks to the community who appreciated it.

Third and Fourth Grade

When I started third grade, my parents moved me back home since I was old enough to help with farm chores. My introduction to public school was at a brand-new building named Ebenezer Elementary School that was next-door to my family's church. I completed my third and fourth grade years in that school. The local school board built this school from the ground up, adjacent to Ebenezer Methodist Church, which is my family's ancestral church. The pastor's home (parsonage) was directly behind the church and the school. Due to its proximity to the school, the church was supportive of and involved in many of the school events.

Ebenezer Elementary School represented a proud moment for the Black community. It was during my time at this building that I first recognized the value of community. I became aware that the people there shared similar values and worked for similar things. Over the years, our community preserved that important historical building. In fact, since attending over 60 years ago, that building, like me, has advanced to senior status. It is now a senior citizens' home … still serving my generation. Thanks to the community!

Middle School Years

Starting in the fourth grade, I completed my elementary and middle school education in the town of Lamar, South Carolina, at Spaulding Elementary School, due to the local school board rezoning students in my parents' neighborhood to attend the schools in town.

My Pre-Teen Years

Puberty is like a caterpillar turning into a butterfly.
It is nature's way of preparing us for adulthood.[17]

> **"Puberty is like a caterpillar turning into a butterfly. It is nature's way of preparing us for adulthood."**

Our family had a culture of work that was so firmly established that I didn't know there was any other way to live. Hard work was one of the core values in our household. I often heard the saying that "hard work never hurts anybody." What they were telling me was that hard work makes you more determined, responsible, and mature. I also noticed that society appreciates and rewards a job that is well done and supported by a good attitude. Life has taught me that hard work is the engine that drives you to be the best you can be and is most often the best pathway to success. I think watching my father and other family members working hard to achieve their goals in life was the thing that influenced me to go into business for myself. I saw firsthand the rewards of becoming an entrepreneur. Even though the work was hard, and there were challenges, I also found out that hard work coupled with prayer works to my benefit, and that has been a strong moral compass for me.

When I was born, my father was a sharecropper. However, over the years he worked hard and saved well. With help from a very liberal local bank, Dad was able to buy his own farm in 1957.

In addition to growing the typical Southern crops (cotton and tobacco), Dad grew vegetables that he sold on a weekly route in his pickup truck to the Black neighborhoods in the small towns near us. He also sold vegetables to grocery stores. Eventually, he opened his own roadside vegetable stand, modeled after his own father's community store. With the expansion of his businesses, he was able to provide jobs for people in our community. Later, my Dad was able to take his savings, plus loans from family members and community friends along with another bank loan, to build and operate a state-inspected butcher shop.

Dad's shop slaughtered hogs and cows for families as well as for businesses. Dad expanded the butcher shop to include a storefront, where he sold cut meats as well as vegetables to both retail and commercial customers. Locals would say that Mr. Lynn's sausage was the best in town. The commercial customers included schools, restaurants, convenience stores, and even military bases. Several of my uncles on both sides of my family also had businesses that included janitorial services, mechanical garages, mowing services, and tractor grading services. Using his own equipment, one of my grandfathers even provided contract harvesting of wheat, corn, and cotton. I credit these examples of my family's drive for business to bringing out the "entrepreneurial gene" in me that led to me building my own family-owned business that has been operating for forty years.

My childhood jobs included slopping the hogs, hoeing weeds, suckering tobacco, picking cotton, putting in tobacco, and harvesting vegetables. My favorite fun-time activity was fishing barefoot in the nearby creek. It was a simple life … filled with family, faith, and love. Our Christian home was led by my father and nurtured by my praying mother. I can summarize my childhood home as one where Daddy was boss, Momma was teacher, and Jesus was King!

Faith was evident in every area of our family's lives. It was this gift of faith that brought me through tough times and helped me celebrate the good times. My life, though simple, was not dull. As a young boy growing up, I was involved in various organizations, such as the 4-H Club, the Boy Scouts, and the New Farmers of America (the organization for African American students similar to the Future Farmers of America). These organizations not only taught me valuable life skills but also gave me wonderful memories that I will always cherish. In fact, it was because of my local and state 4-H Club awards and recognition that a few years later I won a horticulture scholarship that helped me pay my way to Clemson University.

High School Years
Hard Work Without Talent Is a Shame,
But Talent Without Hard Work Is a Tragedy![18]

"Hard Work Without Talent Is a Shame, But Talent Without Hard Work Is a Tragedy!"

One thing that is certain in this life is that change is going to come. As I grew into my teens, I witnessed some very trying times. The headlines were filled with talk of segregation, discrimination, efforts at integration, evolution, revolutions, gun control, and with these the sound of soul music. Our generation was the first to hear of governments shooting rockets to the moon. Things were happening so fast that our elders felt we Baby Boomers were growing up too soon. Across racial lines, my generation was protesting about civil rights and the Vietnam War. The Temptations, a popular singing group, captured many of the troubles of our times in a soulful song called "Ball of Confusion."[19] Soul singer Marvin Gaye also addressed the signs of the times in his hit "What's Going On?"[20] Soul singer Edwin Starr protested the Vietnam War in a #1 hit song entitled "War."[21] These songs were played on the radio so much that the lyrics were always ringing in my head.

The simple, stable life I had at home helped me keep balance in my life while it seemed as if much of the world was going crazy. In addition, my involvement in the 4-H Clubs, the New Farmers of America, and the Boy Scouts reinforced the strong work ethic taught in my home and helped to shape my worldview as well. My commitment to helping my father in his business and furthering my education did not give me much time for social activism. I was supportive of the Civil Rights Movement and desired for changes to be made that were necessary for the educational and economic improvement of our community. However, what I came to realize was that each of us had a job to do; I knew that my involvement in looking for ways to raise the standards of living in our largely rural community was the part I had been given. The organizations that I was involved in were constantly working on ways that farmers could work smarter and yield better crops. My K-12 education reflects and verifies an old Japanese proverb: "Better than a thousand days of diligent study is one day with a great teacher." I had some great teachers, too many to mention, who loved the community we lived in and wanted to see all the people live better.

My Teen Years
We Shall Overcome
Fight for the things that you care about,
but do it in a way that will lead others to join you.[22]

My high school years coincided with local and national movements to integrate public schools. Due to threats of financial and even physical retribution, there was a rush by many of the people in our community to leave the South. Locals would say they were "going up the road." They went to northeastern states like New York, Connecticut, New Jersey, and Washington D.C., to get away from what was going on in the South and to get better paying non-agricultural jobs. There was also a migration to cities in the Midwest like Chicago and Detroit.

African American music played an important role in the Civil Rights effort. Freedom songs were used to highlight the Civil Rights Movement, the best known of which was "We Shall Overcome." However, many popular Black musicians, like Sam Cooke, Aretha Franklin, Billy Holliday, and the Temptations, had songs that were also associated with the Civil Rights Movement. There was a comparable renunciation of the status quo in America in the music of many young White people with musicians like Joan Baez and Bob Dylan, who had songs that were adopted as freedom songs. Young Black men and women in my generation listened and danced to these freedom songs for entertainment and for encouragement.

My high school years coincided with the height of the Civil Rights Movement. By then, songs like "We Shall Overcome" faded into the background as my generation began singing, "Say It Loud, I'm Black and I'm Proud![23] In fact, it seemed as if all music began to reflect a new era. Soul music captured a solid place in the music market. The words to many of the songs reflected the expressions of how Black people felt about the inequality that existed in the institutional and cultural life in the United States. During the sixties, Black radio stations sprung up in towns and cities everywhere. There was at first a noticeable distinction between Black music and White music. However, by the time I finished high school, White artists had begun singing Black music, and Black artists were singing White music. Music was one medium that clearly expressed the cultural changes taking place in this country.

There were many other memorable things that occurred in my life during the 1960s and 1970s; some things I wish I had never witnessed. The television provided us daily with live views of vicious dogs chasing Black people as well as the torrents of water from hoses turned on protestors who were marching peacefully in the public square. These cries for injustice were drowned out by the shouting voices of White onlookers. Not only were these occurrences common in the street, but I also saw homes in my community that had been shot up by the Ku Klux Klan. One thing that was interesting was that even though there were many civil rights protests in the South, there were few race riots involving large-scale fights between the races during civil rights protests in my area. This was unlike what we saw happening up north or on the west coast. Even though the sounds were vicious, the Southern state police or military National Guard units typically maintained reasonable efforts with crowd control.

Before I entered college, throughout the nation, civil rights protests had intensified. However, when I began at Clemson University, one thing was evident; there were no demonstrations going on there. However, less than 200 miles away from Clemson at South Carolina State College, three Black students were killed and 28 were injured by gunfire from White police officers during a bonfire protest in front of the SC State campus. This event drew national attention and was called the Orangeburg Massacre. This incident occurred because of students protesting after a Black Vietnam veteran had been denied service in a local segregated bowling alley. As a Black Clemson freshman, I found myself sometimes a little concerned with the thought that I was one of approximately 25 Black students on a campus of approximately 6,300 White students. My thoughts were, "I'm in trouble if what happened at South Carolina State happens at Clemson."

I also gave some thought to those students who actively protested and broke down barriers, creating opportunities for Black people across the nation. By the time I graduated from Clemson in 1970, I realized these SC State students and Jackson State College (Mississippi) students had lost their lives protesting for the civil rights of Black citizens. Ironically, President Lyndon Johnson made reference to my own home state of South Carolina in the Civil Rights Act, which he signed into law in 1964. This law was intended to end segregation and discrimination in public schools and public accommodations. These efforts no doubt paved the way for integration to occur at Clemson.

When I entered Clemson, an atmosphere of racial reconciliation existed, and it was as if the Lord had ordered my steps to attend a school where I was part of a movement that had already begun to open doors to bring integration of the races. I also saw that by going to a school that cooperated in the integration of the races, I was also a vital part of the goal of the Civil Rights Movement. In terms of my personal development, attending an integrated school helped me assimilate with people with whom I otherwise would not have had the opportunity to do so. For as an African American male, I studied together with White males, and we learned from each other and learned to respect one another. We discovered that in our season of life we were focusing on the same goals, to make life better for ourselves and for others. In the process, we made lifelong friendships. As I reflect on that time of my life, I know now that my attendance at Clemson was a valuable part of breaking down the walls of segregation and building bridges of racial harmony. That time provided us with the opportunity for both Black and White students to become leaders of racial reconciliation in our generation. *Look at God!*

EDUCATION, A PANACEA FOR A BROKEN WORLD

I agree with the statement that education is a vaccine for ignorance and bad behavior as well as a passport to success. My parents obviously instilled that belief in me and made sure that the schools I attended supported this belief too. Thus, the schools I attended not only stressed essential academic skills but also reinforced the moral and Christian values that my family believed in. After my family, the community of the small town of Lamar, South Carolina was an important part of my life. The elders of my community were concerned about my generation going further in life than they had been able to while growing up.

These factors created the environment that shaped me into the person I am today. I give credit to all these people and institutions, recognizing that by God's grace, I was always in the place that God intended for me to be in, to walk into the future that He had in mind. In our way, those of us who chose to be involved in integrating schools and universities were the "first" in many things. This paved the way for others to come behind us without facing the same struggles. My life lesson as spoken so eloquently by Dr. Martin Luther King Jr. during the Civil Rights movement: "The time is always right to do what is right."[24] It was right for me to go to Clemson, right for me and right for the generations who came behind me.

CHAPTER 4

CARS ARE IMPORTANT TO A GUY! DRIVING DURING MY TEEN YEARS

From a Mule to a Tractor to the Family Car

During my teen years, I was anxious to get a driver's license so that I could go places of my own choosing. In South Carolina, the legal age for daytime driving was 15 years old. This enabled those of us on the farm to drive vehicles, and my father encouraged my driving for this reason. It was because of my experience driving on the farm that I became a good driver.

My first driving experience occurred when I was 8-10 years old with my Daddy's mule, Daisy. I directed Daisy with ropes on a halter as she pulled a sled used to haul freshly cropped tobacco leaves from the fields to the barns to be strung on sticks for curing. Young boys like me couldn't keep up with "croppers" and were often assigned to drive the sleds beside the cropping crews until they were filled with tobacco leaves. At the curing barn, the drivers swapped the full sled for an empty one to head back to the field. On one occasion, while I was guiding Daisy to be hitched to an empty sled, she kicked me.

Fortunately, the kick did not cause me too much physical damage, but my ego was severely damaged as the predominately female stringer crews at the barn laughed at me. From then on, I knew when and how to avoid being kicked by Daisy. I have used that mule kick incident as wise counsel most of my life. The wisdom that followed me was that the first time a mule kicks you it is the mule's fault; the second time that mule kicks you it is your fault. After all, "there is nothing to be learned from the second kick of a mule."[25]

> **"There is nothing to be learned from the second kick of a mule."**

When my Dad got a tractor, Daisy was replaced. I was chosen to drive the tractor between the field and barn, just as I had done with Daisy the mule. When the sleds were upgraded to two-wheeled trailers, I developed the skill to drive and back up those trailers. The skills that I developed maneuvering tobacco trailers was used to win several competitive 4-H tractor driving events, which was another contributing factor to my being awarded a scholarship to Clemson. *Look at God!*

When I turned 15 years old, my Dad encouraged me to get an automobile drivers license. With a driver's license, I could help with other farm chores while adhering to the curfew established by my state of only being able to drive with a "dawn to dusk" restricted driver's license. This kind of license permitted the driver to drive from dawn to dusk so they could help perform chores. Not long after getting my official driver's license, I learned that nothing improves a man's driving like being innocent and followed by a police car. My assigned tasks now included going to local towns to pick up supplies, equipment, and spare parts, or even to pick up day laborers. While going back and forth, I had time to think. Eventually, my entrepreneurial mindset kicked in, and on weekends I would load up the pickup truck with watermelons to sell as I was parked beside main roads leading into local towns. I especially used this roadside parking strategy to sell watermelons to stock car race fans coming to the stock car race events like the Southern 500 at the Darlington Raceway, which was near my Dad's farm. For most of my high school years, I created my allowance from the sale of fresh fruit and vegetables. *Look at God!*

When I turned 16 years old, I passed the test for an unrestricted driver's license to become an SC School Bus Driver, which meant earning a monthly wage. During my high school days, the most popular kids were the athletes and the bus drivers. Due to farm chores, I was not allowed to try out for a school sports team. Therefore, my bus driving gig allowed me to stay in the ranks of the POPULAR kids with the bonus of also getting PAID. *Look at God!*

DRIVING DURING MY YOUNG ADULT DAYS
From a Clunker Car to a Muscle Car

When I went to college, Clemson didn't allow freshmen to have cars. Frankly, my family could not have afforded a car for me anyway. I had to catch rides back and forth from college with upper classmen for trips home on the weekend or holidays. By the time I was a college senior, I'd saved enough money from my Advanced ROTC stipend and by working in the campus dining hall to get an old Ford Falcon station wagon. The station wagon was not fancy, but I was able to leverage that car to increase my popularity since I had wheels! Having graduated in 3.5 years with a BS degree and a commission as an Army 2nd Lieutenant, I got a deferment from active duty and enrolled in an MS degree program. I also got a Graduate Assistant Fellowship, which I used to upgrade my Falcon station wagon to a newer car. A car dealer in my hometown knew my Dad well and agreed to sell me a newer car on credit with my Dad's guarantor signature. I chose a popular muscle car, a 1970 Chevrolet SS-396.

When I graduated with my MS degree, I got another military deferment to continue in school to pursue a PhD at the University of Maryland. Even though it was a gas-hog, the SS-396 was a reliable car for my frequent trips between College Park, Maryland, and Darlington, SC. Again, the muscle car increased my popularity with fellow students.

MY ADULT DRIVING DAYS
From Mule to Land Yacht

Audrey and I got married while I was in grad school at the University of Maryland. After we had our first child, we decided to get a more sedate family car, so we traded the SS-396 for a lesser muscle car, an Oldsmobile Cutlass 442, for me and a minivan for her. My love of muscle cars declined as my love for my wife and child grew.

After earning my PhD, I took a job as a field representative with a major agrichemical company. That industry job included a company car that I could use for limited personal use. Audrey drove the Olds 442, and I drove my company car, a full-sized Ford station wagon, so we got rid of the minivan. As my career progressed in various corporate jobs, I chose fancy pickup trucks instead of station wagons. The pickup trucks satisfied and fed my childhood love for pickup trucks, which were the kind of vehicles I drove when I first learned to drive. Since I started my own business, I have always kept a personal pickup truck in the driveway in addition to a family car or SUV. My wife's traditional sedan cars gradually gave way to smaller SUVs as they gained popularity beginning about 2008.

As my business was growing, I often made sales calls on potential customers. In the late 1990s, after marketing to a client for a year, that customer selected my firm for a large five-year grounds' maintenance contract. When I met with that client, he shared information about the notice of award and offered me some business advice. The client told me that his team noticed that I typically drove old beat-up pickup trucks or my family minivan when I called on his organization. He said that based on the vehicles that I drove; the contract evaluation team had some concerns about my ability to afford the start-up costs of this large contract. Of course, they eventually required that all shortlisted bidders submit mobilization plans along with supporting financial stability statements. Having a good relationship with a business banker was helpful as he provided proof and confidence that I'd be able to meet the financial obligations associated with the contract. That client eventually developed a mentoring relationship with me and recommended that I drive vehicles that represented some level of success, i.e., that I could afford a fancy vehicle. Soon after that discussion, I started leasing full-sized SUVs every two years, and potential clients seemed to notice the difference.

For the past 20 years, I've leased or purchased luxury SUVs as my company car. A few years ago, after that client retired, he told me that the logic behind his recommendation was that a fancy vehicle suggests that a vendor has achieved a certain level of success. I now tell young business owners that my high-end luxury SUVs signal to clients that I'm reasonably successful and that I'm probably not cheap. I humbly and jokingly call my high-end luxury SUV company car my LAND YACHT. I summarize my driving instruments as improving from "a mule to a land yacht." From childhood to now, I have been a safe driver. I've gotten a few speeding tickets over the years, but overall God has kept me safe in my lane. However, my history with cars is a graphic illustration of how God has taught and matured me, because after all, cars are important to a guy.

IT TAKES A VILLAGE TO RAISE A CHILD
MAKING LIFE-CHANGING DECISIONS

*"Train up a child in the way he should go;
even when he is old, he will not depart from it."* (Psalm 22:6)

My wife and I found that raising a child requires unconditional love, consistency, clear guidance, endless giving, a watchful eye, endless patience, thoughtful teaching, careful role modeling, a listening ear, a fair mind, an open heart, and community support. That is exactly what I had as a child and as a young adult. Both my wife and I were able to thrive as young people growing up because we were surrounded by people who recognized the importance of community. As parents, we soon accepted that no one is exempt from generational child raising responsibilities. Each of us has a responsibility and a duty to help raise up the next generation of good parents, good citizens, good leaders, and good CHRISTIANS. However, for them to "BE ONE that is good, they've got to SEE ONE." Even if we attempt to save only one child from making bad decisions, while it may not change the world, for that one child … their world will be changed forever.

Currently, we are looking at a generation that has so many opportunities to become successful, and yet there are relatively few people who are willing to invest in helping them determine which opportunities they should take and then help them navigate the ones they do choose. When I am in my "grouchy old man" mood, I lament that it's a shame that youth is wasted on the young. Yet many of the things that plague our youth, steering them to a life of poor decisions, could be circumvented through early intervention from parents and strategic involvement from older adults. The

Bible says: *"Discipline your children, and they will give you peace of mind and will make your heart glad"* (Proverb 29:17). Conversely, one of the results of children who have no structure at home or community involvement in their lives is addressed by an old African proverb: "The child who is not embraced by the village will burn it down to feel its warmth." We would all do well to realize that for some children who crave attention, any attention given is better than no attention, even if it is negative.

> **"The child who is not embraced by the village will burn it down to feel its warmth."**

I'm a beneficiary of a village that was willing to get involved with raising me and my peers. As the time came when I needed to decide about my college plans, I pondered over making a decision. I soon found out that, due to the community's involvement in the Civil Rights Movement, my decision was not just my decision to make. The Black church leaders, school leaders, and civic groups in my community rallied together to work for equal educational opportunities for all students, regardless of race, color, or creed. To achieve this, they looked for Black students who could qualify for admission into White schools and who were willing to be trailblazers by integrating those schools. The leaders were willing to engage in this effort to the extent that the students recommended could demonstrate that any Black student who was denied admission would have only been turned away because of their race. I was a good student and could compete academically, with my SAT scores, my attendance, and my extracurricular involvement, as well as any of my White peers. There was therefore no reason that I should not be accepted at any state-funded public college in South Carolina. Initially, I wanted to attend South Carolina State College, anticipating that there I would enjoy college life away from home and be able to play my clarinet in their "hotshot" Marching 101 Band. This was my first choice. However, my school and community leaders urged me to apply for a Clemson scholarship. I then had to rethink my decision. Having heard from a young age the saying, "a bird in the hand is worth two in the bush," I saw the scholarship to Clemson as being in the hand, and along with it came another hand with an invitation to try out for the Clemson Tiger Band. It made sense for Clemson to rise to become my top choice.

Further, by the time I graduated from high school in 1967, notable architect Harvey Gant, who was the first African American to attend Clemson University, had already integrated Clemson in 1965 without racial incident. He had also won acclaim by being an honor student. The rationale behind me attending Clemson was simple. My teachers knew I wanted to receive the education to become a county agent or a 4-H agent. During those days, most South Carolina counties had a Black county extension agent and a White county extension agent. The White county agent was always the lead or the only agent for a county. Almost everyone who served as a lead county agent was a Clemson graduate. With the guidance of many folks in my Village, my decision about my college attendance seemed simple … they helped me to see that it only made sense that I should go to Clemson.

CHAPTER 5

EDUCATION IS THE TIDE THAT LIFTS ALL BOATS

I finally made the decision to give up the part of me that desired a typical college social life to attend Clemson. I was quite unsure of what my experience would look like. The Black teachers at my high school as well as the local leaders in my community believed in me. They knew I would be successful wherever I went. I'm not going to deny that I had apprehension. When you are a young man growing up in a nation where the governor of Alabama stood on the steps of the University of Alabama with dogs to prevent Black students from attending, you can't help but be concerned. Yet it was at that point that the things my Mother and Father had instilled in me reached my heart. I discovered that, when put to the test, my faith was stronger than my fears. I believed in

God, and I believed in the community that believed in me. This gave me the courage day by day to move forward.

Several adages spoke to my heart. The first was something that Mark Twain said, "Courage is resistance to fear but not the absence of fear." That really addressed how I felt. The next thought that came to mind was, that courage is also the price that the Lord expects for granting FAVOR to His children. If I wanted the favor of God, I also had to grab hold of the courage He grants to those who step out on faith to receive it.

FAMILY COLLEGE ATTENDANCE HISTORY
Give a man a fish and you feed him for a day,
teach a man to fish and you feed him for a lifetime.[26]

My elders understood that education is the soul of a society as it passes from one generation to the next. Knowledge is like a garden; if it isn't cultivated, you can't harvest it. At the turn of the 20th century, my great grandparents sent my grandmother on my father's side of the family to college at Allen University in Columbia, SC.

> **"Give a man a fish and you feed him for a day, teach a man to fish and you feed him for a lifetime."**

Grandma and Grandpa Lynn were married in 1918, and they had nine children; my father was the oldest son. As a result of her college experience, Grandma Lynn was apparently the motivation that rallied the family to send their youngest son, Marvin Lynn, to college in 1952. When Uncle Marvin graduated from SC State College, he was also commissioned as a 2nd Lieutenant in the Air Force. After graduating from South Carolina State College, Uncle Marvin went on to Tuskegee Institute in Alabama to become a veterinarian. He saw combat duty as a dog handler during the Korean War.

Ironically, Uncle Marvin's public health job gave him the credibility and firsthand knowledge to be able to help my Dad completely adhere to regulations when he opened his state inspected meat packing plant. *Look at God!* I was impressed with Uncle Marvin, and I was determined to become the next Dr. Lynn in the family. I did become the next Dr. Lynn in 1975, which was 15 years after Uncle Marvin had become Dr. Lynn. In 2004, my youngest daughter Krystal became the next Dr. Lynn in the family, almost 30 years after I had become Dr. Lynn and 45 years after Uncle Marvin had! My testimony to these achievements is, "Look at God; to God be the glory."

I've heard many stories about how my family members struggled to pay for the college education of their children. Not all the relatives in my family were able to choose the route of higher education, but everyone in my family became skilled in the area that they chose to enter into. Whether it was formal or vocational education, we were taught that, in the words of former Harvard President Bok Derek, "If you think education is expensive, try ignorance." Hence, *learning* to do a job was a *precursor* to doing the job. This was coupled with our families' belief that a good, honest day's work on a good, honest job produced success. Training was essential no matter what the career choice.

My College Decision
Follow the Money! [27]

My high school principal, the Black high school teachers, and the Black preachers joined forces in encouraging me to go to Clemson to study agriculture. I was a prime candidate because I not only had the required

"Follow the Money!"

academic preparation, but I also had actual practical experience with agricultural projects. My parents knew that I wanted to be a county extension agent who would go around to help the farmers in the county with improving their crops. The television show *Green Acres,* a sitcom about a county extension agent, made this popular in the late sixties and seventies.

My parents encouraged me to consider all my options, and that included submitting an application to Clemson. I applied to Clemson. And I got accepted. It was then up to me to make a decision. Of course, included in that decision was the question as to whether my parents could afford Clemson's tuition. As God would have it, He had already planned for the tuition question years before. My years of membership in 4-H clubs paid off. My choice for my field of study was horticulture, and during my high school years, I received several state and national 4-H awards and participated in several fruit and vegetable shows. Consequently, a group called the South Carolina Fruit and Vegetable Association gave me a horticulture scholarship, which paid 50% of my tuition.

With the offer of a scholarship, there was no question in my Daddy's mind after that as to where I needed to go. He sat me down and had a good talk with me, teaching me something that I still pass down to students and their families today: *FOLLOW THE MONEY!* It made sense to attend a school where half of my tuition would be paid as opposed to going to a school where I would have to figure out how to pay the full tuition. That made sense to me then, and it still makes sense to me now.

CHAPTER 6

MY YEARS AT CLEMSON

You Can Convince Anyone You Belong
Somewhere If You Act Like You Belong There.[28]

Clemson was the beginning of both my adult journey and my career journey. Up until the time I entered college, my parents oversaw and guided my life's journey, and I submitted to them. In fact, my final decision to go to Clemson versus SC State was largely due to their concerns about finances. My years at Clemson occurred when the push to integrate colleges and universities gained momentum from the 1964 Civil Rights Act. Once I was at Clemson, I adopted one mantra, and all the guys like me shared it: "I could not mess it up for the dudes behind me." African Americans in the South were very cognizant of the changes that were taking place due to federal legislation. It was spoon-fed to us by the older generation how important it was to take these changes seriously. We knew that if we were to cause problems at the school or on jobs, it could very well present a roadblock for other Blacks who would come behind us. We committed to being the best we could be. We didn't see this as having to condescend to being less than anyone else; rather we saw it as a responsibility we should take seriously. By the way, 60 years later, many Black Clemson students still share that mantra. That mantra also meant "paving the way for the students who will enroll after you enrolled."

I know that a lot of things I benefited from came from the hard work of those folks that came before me. As I often say, I know that I received many opportunities by standing on the shoulders of those who came in front of me. This factor made real the wisdom in the statement: Doors opened represent an invitation to come in, but the other purpose of doors is to exclude entry.

As previously stated, we knew that many doors had been closed due to segregation. As doors opened, we saw entry as a privilege and a responsibility. Although I didn't understand everything about the impact our willingness to set an example would make, I realized as I matured with age that I had assumed the role of "a pair of shoulders." Those shoulders were situated so that students following me could stand on them. This was before the terms "paying forward" and "paying back" became popular, but I now know that my efforts were "paying it forward." I utilized and continue to utilize my professional network, my education, and my experience to help the individuals I mentor. I have many examples to substantiate the old saying, "It takes nothing from the light of my candle to use it to light someone else's candle."[29] Additionally, the Bible in 1 Thessalonians 5:11 teaches that we are helpers one to another, and I adhere to that.

"It takes nothing from the light of my candle to use it to light someone else's candle."

I was aware that, even though I was in a safe and peaceful bubble at Clemson, events outside of the college could make it burst at any time. Clemson University is located in a small Southern college town. This town was riding the fence between segregation and integration. When I enrolled in 1967, there 12 African American freshmen in my class and 15-20 African American upperclassmen out of a student body population of 6,057 students. I confess that more than once fear gripped me. For the first time, I was put in a position where I wondered what would happen if the couple dozen of us minority students had to defend our personal or civil rights. We didn't know what we would do if there was a misunderstanding of intentions that resulted in physical conflict. It was not as if something overt had happened, but the general climate of the country during this time generated fear, and it was hard to ignore it.

INTEGRATION WITH DIGNITY![30]

My faith in God and in the community that believed in me gave me the courage I needed to go through each day without anxiety. I believe the reason for that was due to the words of my daily prayer ritual, "Thank you, Lord for waking me up this morning and starting me on my way." It was also reassuring that Clemson had taken a position concerning integration that they called "integration with dignity." The year that I entered college, there was a very hostile environment in many of the colleges and universities throughout the nation, especially in the Southern United States. However, with this simple motto as the governing force at Clemson, many of the things that were happening in those other places did not happen at Clemson.

Deliberations leading up to Congress passing the 1964 Civil Rights Act contributed in part to the nonviolent integration of Clemson University and the University of South Carolina. In 1967, when I entered Clemson, integration was not being challenged. However, it was also due to the administration and Board of Trustees, who did not fight federal laws but embraced them by going one step further in creating a policy giving the integration process "dignity." As I look back on those years, I know that the Lord ordered my steps to be at an institution that elevated integration to a place of dignity. The climate at Clemson was such that I was not only influenced by good people, but I was also able to influence people I went to school with. In addition, I made lifelong friends who have been a blessing in my life because of the Clemson connection.

MY LIFE VERSE

And we know that all things work together for good to them that love God, to them who are the called according to his purpose. Romans 8:28

I worked hard at Clemson, taking extra courses to ensure there would be no question that I would graduate on time. One thing that I missed by going to Clemson was that there were no Black sororities or fraternities in 1967 when I enrolled. There were, however, many memorable redeeming events. I was the third Black member in the Clemson University Tiger Band, and the band welcomed me and the other Black members. More than that, the faculty was supportive. For example, in 1967, I remember that while en route to an away football game, the band stopped at a rural restaurant, and the owner refused to serve the three Black boys present. Our band leader packed everyone back on the bus, and we left. There were no protests and no fanfare, yet it was a real-life application of what it means to have "integration with dignity." I made many White friends while in the band because they realized that I was just like they were, doing the same things they did as teenagers. Playing and traveling with the band was one of my more pleasant college memories.

FOLLOW YOUR CALLING!

The second thing that stood out during my years at Clemson was the benefit of being in a public land grant A&M college. My horticulture course of study only enhanced what I loved to do, which was to work with the land and the things that grew from it. Not all was study, however. Clemson's Black and White students enjoyed the same things at college that we enjoyed at home. We played pickup basketball and football games. Even though the White and Black students did not room together, we lived in the same dormitories, and we ate together and played games together. Another thing we did as a group of country boys was to act on the need to create an agricultural fraternity. In the late 1960s, I was the only Black member of a group of agricultural students who founded the Clemson Alpha Gamma Rho Fraternity. It was some twenty years later when my own daughter went to Clemson that she found out that I was one of the founding fathers of the Beta Zeta Chapter of Alpha Gamma Rho. Some of her classmates teased her, joking that, "Your Dad is the brother who was a brother." I realized then that I did make some valuable contributions during my years at Clemson.

If You Are Not Part of the Solution, You Are Part of the Problem!

There were times of reflection during my college years when I wondered if I was doing enough to further the civil rights struggle, while so many of my peers were. Dr. King had organized sit-ins and other demonstrations throughout the South, and many college students were heavily involved, with some even paying a very high price in the struggle for integration by risking their lives. Trying to further my education to learn as much as I could to make life easier for farmers and subsequently families meant that I didn't always seem to be on the same level as those who were on the front lines picketing or in the trenches staging actual protests at lunch counters and other public places. The inner struggle was real, but ultimately, I came to the conclusion that what I was doing by learning all that I could about horticulture was going to be even more important to families as just laws and practices were put into place.

In my second college semester, Dr. Martin Luther King Jr. was assassinated, and by then there may have been 25 Black students enrolled at Clemson. The university decided to give us several state-owned vans to go to Dr. King's funeral. In 2021, ESPN TV created a film simulation of Clemson giving 10-12 Black students state-owned passenger vans to drive to Atlanta to attend the funeral. Due to the crowd size, we couldn't get into the church for the funeral, so, following the lead of other funeral attendees, we climbed buildings and mounted fire stairs to the top of buildings so we could see what was going on. I appreciated then, and do even more so now, that even in those days Clemson was trying in their way to contribute to the effort to bring harmony among the races. I remember fondly that of the many things going on during the Civil Rights Movement, when it was left to the kids who got involved, we worked things out.

My three and a half years of undergrad study at Clemson and my one and half years in graduate school, for a total of five years, were amongst the best times of my life. We continued with the idea that started out as just a saying among the first Black Clemson students and was treated like a pledge: "Don't mess it up for the dudes behind you." If you were going to be in the band, be a good band member; if you were going to major in chemistry, be a good chemist; if you were going to play basketball, be a good basketball player. And if you are a member of a student organization or a

Greek organization, then "don't mess it up for the dudes behind you." Even today this saying is still has part of the conviction of the Black students at Clemson, for they still say, "don't mess it up for the dudes behind you."

You Better Praise HIM!

I wasn't at Clemson long before I realized that God had positioned me, right where I was, for His purpose, i.e., *"for such a time as this"* (Esther 4:14). When I first started at the school, I realized that there was no one there to make me go to church. My Dad and Mom were leaders in our local church, and they saw to it that we went every Sunday. I made a public profession of faith at the tender age of 12 years old when I committed my life to the Lord as the choir sang "Just As I Am."[31] As a college student, I was no longer under my parents' watchful eye and household rules. However, it was instinctive within me that I should go to church, not because I had to, but because it was what I knew to be right. It was part of me to say my prayers every night and every morning, as I had as a child. Therefore, whether I was in a college dorm, an army barracks, an apartment, a new house in a new town, or a hotel on a business trip, I got on my knees and prayed every night before going to bed and every morning when I got up. This practice continues even until today and has blessed me well throughout my life. My spiritual life has helped me internalize the saying that faith doesn't just make things easier, it makes them possible.

Count Your Blessings, Not Your Problems!

The Civil Rights era coincided with the Vietnam era. There were a lot of White kids my age protesting the war and demanding an end to it. It wasn't long before the conflict over Vietnam overrode the civil rights issue for me in terms of having to make an important decision.

Just as Black Students were killed by police at SC State in 1968 during a civil rights protest, White students at Kent State University were shot and killed while protesting the Vietnam War. Freshman and Sophomore ROTC was mandatory at Clemson based on its legacy of formerly being a military school. When I became a sophomore, I had to decide whether I would just finish my mandatory basic ROTC training or further my training. I decided to become a military officer by going through advanced ROTC during my junior and senior college years.

It was an advantage for me that I really liked the idea of serving in the military. I was advised that I could still get an education and have the advantages of being a part of the Army if I opted to become an officer. Every day, the media was striving to give glory and glamour to the war. This led me into questioning whether it was my patriotic duty to go to Vietnam. My Uncle Marvin had served in the Korean War as an officer and dog handler. Two of my uncles had also served in Vietnam. Our family supported the efforts of the Armed Forces, and I was prepared to go. The military veterans in my family, however, encouraged me to combine higher education with military service. They advised me to complete my education first if possible. Uncle Marvin was a perfect example of how to make the military service–higher education path work. Since he had the titles of Colonel Lynn and Dr. Lynn, I could see that "he had been there, and he had done that." Consequently, I also ended my military service time as Captain Lynn and Dr. Lynn.

A Corporate Career from my Military– Higher Education Training
Two Skill Sets Are Better Than One.

As the time drew near for my graduation from Clemson, I received my commission as a second lieutenant in the US Army Chemical Corp. I believed in Proverbs 11:14, which says, *"in the multitude of counselors, there is safety."* Thus, not only did I seek out sound advice and loving encouragement from my family, but I also got sound advice from military veterans and local leaders in my community.

My Clemson professor of military science also advised me to consider a higher education–military service career track. During an informal discussion after I'd gotten my second lieutenant's commission, his advice was: "Lynn, they don't need any more second lieutenants over there. in Vietnam, they are bringing lieutenants home. Why don't you take advantage of your opportunity here at Clemson and get another degree, and while doing so you can join a reserve unit that will be based near Clemson or whatever college you attend." My motivation to work hard in college always focused on getting as much education under my belt as possible in order to be the best that I could be. I was willing and ready to go to the war if drafted, but until that time I made the decision to concentrate on my education.

After I graduated with my MS degree at Clemson, my military professor continued to advise me. In 1972, when I had an MS degree in my hand, that same professor said to me, "Why don't you go ahead and get a doctoral degree so you can come back here and become a full-fledged professor?" He elaborated that it would also give me an advantage in the military as an officer if I needed it. After giving this thought some prayer, I decided that it was the way I should go.

I was commissioned as a chemical core officer. During those days, Agent Orange and 2,4-D were being used in Vietnam. Since I had training in vegetation management, the idea of getting a doctorate degree was attractive. That academic credential could enable me to not only become a specialist in the military but also a weed control professor. After successfully graduating with my BS and MS degrees from Clemson, on the advice of my professor of military science who had helped me decide to continue my education, I enrolled at the University of Maryland in pursuit of a doctorate. My intention was to return to become a teacher and a professor at Clemson. While at the University of Maryland, I served in an Army Reserve unit in Baltimore. During the early '70s, reservists were called 90-day wonders. This name applied to those in the Reserves who only had to complete 90 days of active duty to qualify for a pension. The Department of Defense was looking for a way to prevent short termers (i.e., those with fewer than 90 days of active duty) from collecting the same military pension plan as those who had served two years and longer. My military career fit into that program as a career reservist who served 89 days of active duty at Fort McClellan followed by 14 years in various Army Reserve units in the towns that I lived in.

I was among those who were trying to fulfill the requirement for active duty as commissioned officers. The established plan was to serve in the reserves on active duty for 89 days. I did those 89 days at Fort McClellan in Alabama. This was the home of the Chemical Corps, which fit my educational plan well. What that meant for me was that I would not only be able to perform my term of duty, but I would also be able to gain valuable experience in the field of study that I had chosen to pursue. My reasoning assured me that it made sense, but I also felt as if my decisions were part of an even bigger plan than I could see at the time.

Graduate College Education – My Years at the University of Maryland

What you get when you accomplish your goals is not as important as what you become by accomplishing your goals.[32]

> **"What you get when you accomplish your goals is not as important as what you become by accomplishing your goals."**

Since I got married while I was in graduate school, my new wife and I needed a house near the University of Maryland campus. We moved into a little house at the University of Maryland's Vegetable Research Farm in Salisbury, Maryland. As a part of my Graduate Assistantship, the University of Maryland also provided married student housing on the main campus in College Park during the school year and at the Vegetable Research

Farm in Salisbury, Maryland, during the summer. We got married in June, and my friends from the University of Maryland came down for the wedding. I knew even then that we were blessed. I had a beautiful wife, a new car, and my assistantship paid us money to live on. I also got paid from the U.S. Army Reserves membership based on my status of being a commissioned officer through Clemson ROTC. Audrey got a job as a librarian on campus. We were off to a great start.

After I successfully defended my PhD dissertation, I turned my efforts to searching for a job. I wanted to be gainfully employed by the time I graduated in May 1975. My wife and my family were looking forward to the PhD hooding ceremony at the College Park Campus at the University of Maryland, and it was a memorable ceremony for me and my loved ones. Coretta Scott King, the wife of the late Reverend Martin Luther King, Jr., was the event speaker. Especially memorable was that Mrs. King personally hooded the PhD candidates and was the first person to call me Dr. Lynn.

I chose to include in my advanced studies the study of weed control and chemical weed control in vegetable and row crops. I give credit to that military–higher education track for opening doors that led to my getting a PhD. That track also led to my successful 15-year corporate career in the agrichemical industry. By taking the advice of my teachers and relatives who were veterans, I was able to successfully navigate a dual education, one that provided me with a PhD and another that provided me with much-needed skills and knowledge through my engagement with the military. Reflecting on this, I again realize that God was directing my steps. *Look at God!*

CHAPTER 7

My Wife – Audrey!

"A happy man marries the girl he loves; a happier man loves the girl he married."[33]

Even with all the good things that were going on in my life as I pursued my doctorate, there was still something missing. It didn't take me long to realize that I needed that pretty girl from my hometown in my life. I decided that I was going to propose to my childhood sweetheart, Audrey, and that's just what I did.

My wife Audrey is my soulmate. We celebrated our 50th wedding anniversary in June of 2023. Proverbs 18:22 says, *"the man that finds a wife finds a treasure and receives favor from the Lord."* This has been my story. Audrey has stood right with me through the many events of our lives, through the good times and the challenging times. She has been the love of my life for two-thirds of my life. We benefit from the bond of marriage in that it has brought two hearts together in ways indescribable. Even during the times we were at our weakest, we found strength in each other. We often prayed that the Lord would protect us from hurt, from harm, and from dangers both seen and unseen. I believe that prayers have been answered over and over again. There are so many memories that we have shared, and looking back on them, they are the best part of my life.

Audrey and I have known each other and been friends most of our lives. We met in elementary school when she was 9 years old, and I was 10. We essentially grew up together since our families lived in the same farming community. My Mother was leader of a community 4-H club, a home economics group. Audrey and her sisters were members of Mom's 4-H club. My Dad was also leader of a community 4-H Club, a livestock group that I was a member of. In fact, Audrey was my first date when several community 4-H clubs held a holiday awards dinner and dance at a local high school gym. Neither of us were old enough to drive, so my Mom picked Audrey up, took us to the dance, and waited for us. When we took Audrey home, I remember that Audrey's Dad cut on the front porch lights as I walked her to the door to say good night. Their dogs chased me back to the car, even though the dogs had seen me frequently because I was from the neighborhood. Today I still joke about that first date, that her Dad had something to do with those dogs chasing me.

Throughout our high school years, Audrey and I dated. When I graduated from high school a year earlier in 1967, she was still my girlfriend. We attempted to keep our relationship going while I was at Clemson. Clemson was quite a way away from our hometown, Darlington, and the long-distance relationship was tough. She graduated a year later and went to an HBCU named Morris College. I would still spend time with Audrey over the summer. However, during the school season, we grew apart because of the distance and the time away from each other. She had gotten into a routine with her life with her friends at Morris College, and I had grown accustomed to my lifestyle and friends at Clemson. However, we were still dating. In fact, when I was in graduate school at Clemson, I gave her a pre-engagement ring as a Christmas present.

During her senior year, Audrey was elected as Miss Morris College in 1972. I always imagined that I'd someday marry a beauty queen, and this peer recognition confirmed that she was indeed not only the girl of my dreams but my beauty queen as well. The bond between us went deeper than the distance between us. I was already in graduate school at the University of Maryland working on my doctorate, so when I came to South Carolina for Christmas 1972, I asked her to marry me. The same jewelry store that sold me the pre-engagement ring helped me pick out an engagement ring. Audrey accepted my engagement proposal, and we started planning for a summer wedding.

The advantage we had as we began to plan for marriage was that her parents approved of me, and my parents loved Audrey like she was one of their own daughters. In our small local town, it was no secret that we had been dating since our teenage years. So as word spread that we were engaged, many of our friends and family said, "I knew that you all would get married someday."

My sisters have always accepted Audrey as their sister. Likewise, Audrey's sisters accepted me like a brother. Throughout our dating years, and even now after so many years of marriage, her only living sister treats me as both a brother and a brother-in-law. Audrey and my sisters are genuine friends as well. From the beginning of our relationship, we have enjoyed doing the same things. Our lives together have been a real family affair. We have years of good times, many memories that I will always treasure, and most of all we have a peace that we have lived within the will of God. *Look at God!*

One of the concerns Audrey and I had early on about marriage had to do with my commitment to the military. I was a commissioned second lieutenant, and the Vietnam war was going on. The question was, would I have to go into full-time active duty in the army to take care of my commitment as a commissioned officer? The Lord blessed us in that our marriage coincided with the Vietnam War winding down, so I was able to fulfill my commitment as an Army Reserve Officer without having to see active duty. I found a reserve unit near the University of Maryland, where I attended a monthly Army Reserve meeting. Active-duty soldiers jokingly referred to reservists like me as "weekend warriors." After I graduated, I still owed several years of military service to the Army Reserves units. For years I attended weekend drill once a month plus an annual two-week summer camp. Even with all the other responsibilities I had, I gave many years to serving my country.

The People Who Light Up My Life Usually Know Where the Switch Is

As newlyweds, we had everything we needed and even some of the things we wanted. At that stage of my spiritual life, my favorite scripture was the twenty-third Psalm. We were living out *"The Lord is my shepherd; I shall not want."* We had housing provided by the university, plus income from my Graduate Assistantship, plus a monthly Army Reserve check. We had a fancy Muscle Car (Chevy SS-396), which was dependable for road trips, and gas cost less than $0.50 per gallon. It was cost efficient for us to make the 400-mile trips on I-95 back to our hometown to visit both of our families and to stock up on groceries. Since my Dad owned a storefront butcher shop, we'd go home every couple of months or so plus holidays. My Mom would pack several ice chests with all kinds of meats plus grocery items. For young people, we felt we were living the good life. While in Maryland we had family near us from Audrey's side, and some of my relatives were also nearby. When we needed encouragement, we had family members from her side and from my side of the family, and they would not only give us encouragement, they sometimes provided a good meal for us too! With so many folks praying with and for us, you could say that we were blessed and highly favored.

We were both from rural South Carolina, but the places where we lived in Maryland in our early years of marriage, while near D.C., were a lot like home. We also had enough access to city life to learn what big city life was like. When I started my career in Corporate America, that city experience paid off. Additionally, during the summer months, we lived in a rural area at the University of Maryland Vegetable Research Farm in Salisbury that was very familiar to us. We had our first child, a daughter, while we were in Salisbury, Maryland, and both of our mothers came to see us when she was born. While I studied and worked on my PhD, Audrey was by my side, encouraging me; she chose to be a stay-home mom. With everything we faced, we faithfully prayed together to God that everything was going to be alright. We settled into a routine; while I was studying, Audrey was being a Mommy for our daughter. As a couple we had the advantage of knowing each other very well, so we both knew all the things each other liked and didn't like. We both loved the relationship our respective parents had with each other, and we modeled that, so in many ways our life was like being home again. Audrey has always been one of my best friends. Knowing each other as friends, and through the years as girlfriend and boyfriend, made our marriage so much easier. During those times when we saw that we needed space, we each went to our own corners, enjoying even more our coming back together.

AUDREY IS THE WIND BENEATH MY WINGS

There are many things I can say about Audrey, but perhaps one that comes to mind most is that she provides me with graciousness, forgiveness, and love. She has been the undergirding strength in my life. I can say, like Solomon did in Solomon 3:4, *"I have found the one whom my soul loves."* God has so wonderfully provided wisdom and guidance in our relationship, and He has poured out grace and mercy in such a way that our love and commitment has been renewed daily. I can honestly say that *"houses and wealth are inherited from parents, but a prudent wife is from the Lord"* (Proverbs 19:14).

The Joy and Benefit of Being Married to My Best Friend For Most of My Adult Life
*The greatest joy in my life has come from
being married to my best friend.*

Of all the things that I have accomplished, none of them would have meant as much to me had I not had Audrey to share them with. God's light has certainly shone down upon our marriage. We learned early that spouses who are intimate, with an emotionally supportive, trusting, and caring relationship, have healthy marriages. We have been friends most of our lives, and we have made it intentional to always be friends, not just husband and wife. We have spent quality time together and learned to appreciate and respect our differences.

My position as a husband focused on taking seriously the scripture from Ephesians 5:33, *"each one of you also must love his wife as he loves himself."* This Bible verse, as well as many others concerning marriage, reveals that men should love their wives as themselves, a commitment that speaks to the deep regard that a husband should have for his wife. Because of frequent moves during our years in Corporate America, we never had time to develop a close set of friends. The decision we made in the raising of our children was to choose relationships with like-minded families wherever we lived. Over the years, we have tried to maintain friends and social business associates who shared our faith.

"Happy wife, happy life."

There is a popular phrase, "happy wife, happy life."[34] I can give evidence that this is true. Recently, I came upon one study by researchers from Rutgers University and another by the University of Michigan that take the statement further. They concluded that the happier a wife is with her marriage, the happier the husband is about his life. What that attests to is that love is a choice we make every day.

Jealousy and resentment are unhealthy emotions, and they punish the person who carries them. Audrey and I diligently work through our disagreements, not going to bed angry or waking up angry. After more than 50 years of marriage, we continue to pray that *"the Lord will increase our love for each other and for everyone else."* (1 Thessalonians 3:2). Our advice to couples is to give your marriage time to work, for time gives you a chance to rethink heated arguments and see them as issues that can be resolved. Given enough time, almost everything can be healed. The second most important thing is to make a commitment, just as Ruth told Naomi in Ruth 1:16-17, *"Where you go, I will go, and where you stay, I will stay."*

Lord Bless Our Marriage Through Sickness and Health

We prayed for it and have lived to see how the Lord has blessed our union. Growing up, I would see my parents praying in many situations; that included bedtime prayers, blessing meals, public prayers in church, and even

"We prayed for it and have lived to see how the Lord has blessed our union."

in their private prayer closets. As a young boy, I learned the twenty-third Psalm and would proudly quote it. *"The Lord is my shepherd"* took on more meaning as I matured. It has helped our marriage survive the test of time. Every time I attend a wedding, I am particularly reminded of the vow I made so long ago: "Do you, Louis, take Audrey to be your lawfully wedded wife? To have and to hold, in sickness and in health, in good times and not so good times, for richer or poorer, keeping yourself unto each other for as long as you both shall live." Our marriage has certainly experienced all the issues spoken during our initial vows, but we have not wavered in our commitment to each other.

As we are now in our senior citizen days, we respond to the parts of our marriage vows with a more realistic focus on "in sickness and in health." This became our focus when Audrey was diagnosed with cancer. After a year of chemotherapy and radiation treatments, her cancer is now in remission. During that season of our lives, however, Audrey's mantra was "GOD's Got THIS!" We had T-shirts printed with that mantra, which we gave to other cancer patients. During that season of our lives, I prioritized caregiver duties over business, boards, and civic/social events. We found strength in our faith. I tell observers that I know she would have done the same for me. We now say that her TEST has become her Testimony.

CHAPTER 8

My First Job, My Career

Industry Versus Academia

In 1975, I found more job opportunities in the agrichemical industry than at research universities. Based on my PhD research on the development of a weed control chemical for use on row crops and vegetables, the Agrichemical Division of Eli Lilly Pharmaceutical Company hired me to do similar work on commercial products that they were developing. While working on my PhD, I had gained familiarity with industry research, which is referred to as "product development."

"Your talent determines what you can do. Your motivation determines how much you are willing to do. Your attitude determines how well you do it."

My decision to work in industry versus academia was more driven by the difference in pay between university and industry scientists. In the mid-1970s, agrichemical companies were paying up to 25% more for entry-level PhD scientists than universities were paying. Since I was married and had a child when I graduated, my decision was in large part driven by finances.

My Corporate Jobs

Your talent determines what you can do. Your motivation determines how much you are willing to do. Your attitude determines how well you do it.[35]

Following is an overview of the jobs that I had before I went into business for myself.

ELANCO
Indianapolis – Home Office Support

As soon as I was awarded my PhD, I accepted a product development job with ELANCO, which is the Agrichemical Division of Eli Lilly Pharmaceutical Company. I was located in their Midwest Regional office so as to learn protocol and policies for ELANCO field research and laboratory research.

ELANCO
Indianapolis – Field Research Scientist Territory

My job as a research scientist for Eli Lilly required me to collaborate and work with university scientists in an assigned territory. My territory included Michigan State, Purdue, Ohio State, and the University of Kentucky.

MONSANTO
St. Louis

After about three years with ELANCO, a scientist from a company called Monsanto contacted me at a trade show where I was presenting a paper that had been written in collaboration with an academic scientist. Monsanto was in the product development phase of the weed control product called Roundup, which is still one of the best-known weed killers. The job offer they made me would pay more money, and I would get to work on developing a novel weed control product. I was first assigned to the Monsanto headquarters in St. Louis to become familiar with in-house product development protocol.

MONSANTO
Syracuse

After about two years, Monsanto moved me to Syracuse, New York, to serve as product development representative for the New England states. My primary product development focus was on fruits and vegetables, especially apples. I had research and grant responsibility with weed scientists at Cornell University, University of Massachusetts, University of Rhode Island, University of Maine, University of Vermont, and University of Connecticut. Personally,

Audrey and I found it difficult to adjust to the winter weather in that area, especially the snow. I remember jokingly telling my Mom that the area had three seasons—June, July, and Winter!!

MONSANTO
Denver

As interest grew surrounding Roundup herbicide, Monsanto decided to split their West Coast product development region into two. The region was west of the Rockies and was split north and south into Denver South to Texas and Denver North to the Northwest States up to the Canadian border. This was my first corporate management position. I was assigned as the PD manager for Denver North with six Monsanto field scientists reporting to me. It was a great career move. However, our family issues about dealing with cold weather and the distance from home (South Carolina) were even further exaggerated.

MONSANTO
St. Louis

After two years in Denver, the company promoted me back to St. Louis as product development manager. I was specifically assigned as PD manager for LASSO herbicide, which was the company's premier weed control product for row crops like corn, soybeans, and cotton.

MONSANTO
Columbia

After about three years as a home office product development manager, a field product development representative position came up in Columbia, South Carolina. I knew that the SC field rep was retiring, so I applied for that job. Even though my current position was several levels above it, I was chosen for the job. Monsanto management knew that I wanted to move back home to South Carolina. The company didn't reduce my salary and paid for the move. Personally, returning to Columbia, South Carolina, was great for us because we were close to our family. The universities in my territory included Clemson and NC State University. As a Clemson graduate, I already knew many of the agricultural scientists in South Carolina and North Carolina. I was that "Local Boy Done Good" model at Clemson because I was a research scientist for Monsanto and had a big research-grant budget. With Monsanto's research checkbook, I gave grants to and worked with some of the professors that I had studied under while at Clemson. It was a great move. *Look at God!*

Family Impact of Relocating

Move #1 – When I accepted the Eli Lilly job in Indianapolis, Audrey and I wanted to become homeowners, so we purchased a condo. It was a condo that Audrey loved. I knew I was going to be traveling, so we intentionally chose a condo in a child-friendly and safe area. Indianapolis introduced us to winter weather and snow, which we'd never experienced. While I was working for Eli Lilly in Indianapolis, we had our second child, another daughter.

Move #2 – Since we knew that the assignment was temporary, we rented a house while we were in the St. Louis headquarters product development training job.

Move #3 – The move to Syracuse, New York, was a promotion. Even so, being from the Deep South, we were genuinely concerned about the harsh winter weather and snow that we had heard about. Nevertheless, we moved and lived there for about two years. From our time in Syracuse, we confirmed that we were not cold weather people.

Move #4 – When we moved to Denver, Audrey selected a house—our first real house in a neighborhood she really loved. For the first time since being out of school, we had a real house in suburbia. We also made new friends and found a good church to attend. It was a good experience for us, finding a neighborhood we both loved and a Black church we also loved. We got another opportunity to experience suburban living because we lived in a totally middle-class suburban neighborhood in Denver. From the standpoint of staying connected with our extended family, it was still difficult to drive back and forth to South Carolina. Denver also had some of the same cold weather features that we had experienced in Syracuse.

Move #5 – When we were transferred back to St. Louis, we purchased a house in a suburban middle-class neighborhood. We were familiar with greater St. Louis, so we knew where we wanted to live. At the time of the move, we anticipated that I'd be a long-term home office manager. We were able to re-establish prior friendships.

Move #6 – While in Columbia, we had our third child. It was eight years from when we had our second daughter, who was born in Indiana. My friends, and especially my Daddy, teased me that I should have named that boy MAC for "middle-aged carelessness." From my viewpoint, things were going well. Then, Monsanto wanted to promote me and move me again. Audrey and I both decided that we did not want to move again. We told them we did not want to take the promotion.

TURNED DOWN RELOCATION OPPORTUNITY from COLUMBIA – After a few years, I was offered a job that required us to relocate from Columbia. After prayer and much discussion, Audrey and I assessed our situation, and I knew that it was time to leave my good corporate job rather than relocating again. Audrey and I decided that South Carolina was the place we were most comfortable.

CHAPTER 9

IMPACT OF RELOCATIONS ON FAMILY LIFE

Be Ready for Opportunities …
In Fact, Chase Opportunities!

Audrey agreed with me concerning staying put with no more moves. She saw the complications to our lifestyle with a corporate career. In some respects, the moves were great, giving us some different experiences around the country. Financially, the moves were also good for us because our moves occurred during the days when corporate headquarters offered very good corporate relocation allowances. We used those corporate relocation allowances plus increases in home equity to purchase homes when we relocated. With the profits that we made from our homes with each sale, we were able to get bigger and better homes with every move.

A major consideration in that decision to stay in South Carolina, however, was that our kids were getting ready to attend school. As young parents, we were unsure about how prior moves had impacted them. Reflecting now on those moving experiences, in a sense they were good for the kids. The adjustments they had to make made them socially flexible and able to adapt to new environments. Nonetheless, with all the reasons we thought staying in South Carolina was a better decision, it was still a tough decision because the corporate job paid very well. Once we made the decision, we were confident that it was right for us.

STARTING MY OWN BUSINESS: FAMILY LIFE
You can't be successful in business without taking risks.

After careful consideration, with determination, we agreed that we should start a business. The cornerstone of my business was that I started out chasing a vision, not the money. I later found out that if the planning and purpose are good, then the money will follow. We took a leap of faith and started a commercial landscape firm. We knew that *"faith doesn't make things easier; it just makes them possible"* (Luke 1:37). After the deep recession of the early 1980s, there was a 15-year economic expansion beginning in 1982, now called "the long boom" by economists. My experience working in Corporate America taught me some valuable things. One was to look at economic forecasts and try to determine what steps I needed to personally take in order to be financially solvent.

Therefore, one of the things I had to consider when the question came up as to whether or not to start a business was whether the market was favorable or not to what I wanted to do. With a great many new construction projects taking place on corporate campuses that were being built, I knew that they would need landscaping. In addition, I saw that there was a growing market for multi-family housing. It was a time when corporations and government agencies were outsourcing landscape services. We determined that offering privatized commercial landscape services represented a growth market. My PhD in horticulture gave me unique credentials and credibility among companies who were looking for learned experts that could determine long-range solutions to their landscaping needs.

My new business only served commercial clients. We only served residential clients when we took on an all the properties in a homeowners' association with at least 25 properties. My only single-home residential customer is my personal house. We took a risk to avoid most residential landscaping and concentrate on commercial landscaping. That risk paid off as the marketplace noticed our ability to service large-acreage commercial customers. Eventually, our list of completed projects enhanced our resume and provided a great "word of mouth" marketing platform. This approach verifies that "Whenever you see a successful business, someone once made a courageous decision."[36]

> **"Whenever you see a successful business, someone once made a courageous decision."**

THE S*tart*-*up* P*lan*
"If you fail to plan, then you are planning to fail."[37]

Once I had created my business, my next challenge was to search out and hire good people to work in the business. It was important for me to hire people who reflected my values and business style. My most important hires were the managers since they would have the responsibility of executing the business plan on a day-to-day basis. My managers were also given the responsibility of seeing that every phase of the business ran smoothly. Initially, I hired three managers who also performed some tasks with crews; I called them "player-coach managers." My first lead manager was a long-term manager in my Dad's butcher shop, so I knew I could trust him to oversee all the necessary tasks while I was marketing the company. With a management team in place, I rented a warehouse and hired some full-time hourly guys to perform day-to-day landscape and lawn care services. I bought a couple of trucks, some lawn mowers, and some handheld equipment when we landed a couple of big corporate lawn maintenance cutting contracts. The big corporate contracts helped to develop my company's reputation. During those early days, when many individuals were venturing out as entrepreneurs, I did a great deal of reading and determined that the best way to ensure success was to plan well.

As the Cheshire cat said to Alice in Wonderland, "If you don't know where you're going, any road will lead you there." I took advantage of business development training offered by agencies like the Chambers of Commerce, small-business development agencies, universities, and trade groups. The knowledge I gained from the workshops and classes I took from organizations like this made it crystal clear to me that a dream written down with a date becomes a goal and that a goal broken down into steps becomes a plan. And finally, that a plan backed by action makes your dreams come true.

I've attributed my success in business to:

1. First, I have done a great deal of reading across a wide range of topics. I wanted to be kept abreast of the latest trends and business strategies. This practice has enhanced my personal ability to problem-solve, but it has also impressed potential clients with my broad range of knowledge on a variety of topics.

2. Second, I have always sought out leaders in whatever field I was venturing into. I have never been timid about taking advice from those who have more knowledge in an area than I have. I learned early in this business that there is always someone who knows more than you do. Taking advice from those more knowledgeable and more skilled is a wise decision for any up-and-coming business.

3. Third, whatever I set out to do, I take a great deal of time to prepare. In fact, I tend to overprepare so that I am potentially able to deal with even unexpected challenges. Preparation has been one of my keys to success. Taking the time to lay out the plan, look for potential challenges, and talk it over with my staff has saved me from making blunders that could have been costly.

To sum it up, these have been my three major practices as a businessman:

1. Reading.

2. Association with people smarter than me.

3. Overpreparing.

Going Into the Marketplace
Taking My Wits and My Faith Into the Marketplace
"Here am I, Lord; Send me" (Isaiah 6:8)

Using my experience in Corporate America, I developed a marketing plan for my business. My kids now say that my folksy style kind of works. As I said earlier, my successes are not all measured in dollars and cents. Influence is much more valuable a measure of success than affluence. When I can influence someone's life, when I'm able to direct them to set forth and attain their goals, therein is the gratification that gives me the most reward. Even in my day-to-day business dealings where I am able to offer someone a job, a paycheck, extended training, a helping hand, or a shoulder to lean on, I have opportunity to share the keys as to how God has blessed my business. That influence is more significant to me than any affluence. This is what fulfills my desire for the Lord to use my life.

I don't judge my business and civic associates. I can't judge them. I avoid friends who judge me by my possessions. I believe in the saying "birds of a feather flock together." I enhance that saying with my belief that "chickens and buzzards come home to roost!" Since my Dad was a butcher, one of his job performance directives, which also doubled as a wisdom nugget, was that if you wallow with pigs, expect to get dirty. Plus the pigs enjoy it.

I believe this kind of wisdom has helped me many times when people need an ear to talk to. People also serve as listeners when I need a listening ear. I seem to be attracted to friends who are what I call Prayer Warriors. These friends are Prayer Warriors for the marketplace and for our families, friends, and loved ones. I've become friends with many pastors, including my current pastor. At this stage of my life, my wife, my children, my sisters, my trusted advisors, and my church family are the strongest relationships in my life. I pray with my church family and with my children. I'm offering my adult children the same foundation that my parents offered me. I want them to see me as a praying man. Never do I part company with my children or grandchildren without us holding hands and praying together

Business
My Start-up Journey Decision
Open for Business
A big business starts small.

Of course, I wanted my business to be profitable. However, based on what I'd seen of entrepreneurial family and friends, I had a two-pronged goal. I noticed that many successful companies were able to make a difference while also making money. Except for access to capital, I had very little concern as to whether our business would succeed. However, it took a while for me to establish a business relationship with a bank. In the beginning, it seemed like a bank was a place that lent you money if you could prove that you didn't need it! As a benefit of joining business and civic organizations, I acquired a network of progressive leaders who, like me, wanted to contribute to the greater good of their community. I met a bank loan officer who took the time to get to know me and understand my business plan. That bank officer approved an asset line of credit that helped me manage cash flow to grow my business. The bank management became familiar with my business, and they had also become aware of my civic involvement on commissions and boards. Within a few years of being a bank client, I was invited to join that bank's City Advisory Board.

After more years passed, I was invited to join their State Advisory Board, and eventually I became a member of that bank's Corporate Board of Directors. As a corporate director of that bank, I was the voice of small-business clients. I served on the Corporate Board of Directors of BB&T Bank from 2013 until 2019, when it merged with SunTrust bank to become TRUIST Bank. While serving as corporate director at BB&T, I participated in several annual national meetings of Black corporate directors of publicly traded Fortune 500 firms. Over the years, I learned how other trades and industries were regulated and governed as compared to the financial services industry that BB&T Bank was a part of.

As a participant in the annual Black Directors Conferences, my network of business associates spread nationwide. The Black Directors Conferences drew attention to my business, civic, and personal credibility, which led to appointments to the New City Headquarters Board of Trustees of the National Urban

League (NUL) and the Washington DC Board of the National Association of Minority Contractors (NAMC).

My "entrepreneurial bloodline," as I have jokingly referred to my strong passion for business, gave me the faith and confidence to believe that my business would make it. While growing up, Audrey and I had seen many Black families succeed in business while still being part-time farmers. My family's farming history was the genesis of my wanting to study horticulture. Audrey and I grew up in the same neighborhood, and Audrey had witnessed firsthand that my parents and relatives were successful as entrepreneurs. It wasn't that different from her background. Many of her family members were also entrepreneurs. We both agreed that we could handle entrepreneurship because we grew up watching our respective families make it work. It wasn't long before the opportunity arrived, and I knew that I couldn't work on my business and work for Monsanto at the same time, so the morning came that I quit my job.

I had saved up some money, and to add to that, the timing for leaving my job was perfect because the company was downsizing. When I told my manager that I was going to resign, the company offered me a "golden handshake" deal. I had a choice to stay, but if not, I'd get paid one week's salary for every year that I had worked. That golden handshake helped us to have enough money to tide us over during the startup phase of my new business. I received fourteen weeks' pay to help me during the startup of my business. In the meantime, my startup company had enough income that it could afford to pay me a salary. While my salary didn't match my Monsanto salary, we were able to live a similar lifestyle. So, thanks to that golden handshake plus our savings, we were able to move forward and maintain a lifestyle similar to what we were used to.

As my own boss, I liked the benefit that I was totally in control of my time. However, I soon learned that "you can take a day off, but you can't take it back." During my business start-up days, I discovered from the beginning that budgeting was very important to me. There were times when there was too much month left at the end of the money! Just as my Dad had done, I made it a practice to save part of our revenue for future goals. When the lean months came, I was still able to make ends meet because of the cushion I had set aside. This allowed me to continue to care for both my business and my family. There was no doubt that I felt successful when I reached a level of financial security by learning how to budget and harness my resources. After a few years, as my business was growing, I learned several twists about budgeting as follows. Though they may not seem to be specific to budgeting, when I took these principles into my everyday business transactions, they worked for me.

1. On revenue: Make it first; then, make it last.

2. You cannot spend your way out of debt.

3. Expect the best. Prepare for the worst. Capitalize on what comes.

4. The future is never made brighter by burning the candle at both ends.

5. Do things that your future self will thank you for.

6. Don't spend your life chasing money and end up as the richest man in the cemetery.

7. "Eat, Sleep, Hustle, Repeat"—Good things happen to those who hustle.

It's About What You Know and Who You Know!
The Secret of My Success Summed up in Two Words: Know People

Years of working in Corporate America had strengthened my ability to establish and maintain working relationships with all types of people. I learned from my corporate experience that while working on a common project, your success depends on teamwork. I also saw that a major determiner of success is how you interact with your team. Mutual respect develops as you learn to lean in on the different strengths of one another. I also observed that collegiality takes place as you work long hours, eat together, and plan together. As you work together over time, you find out about each other's families and find that we all have our share of ups and downs, sorrows, and joys. These combined experiences enabled me over the years to develop a comradery among my staff, which contributed to developing a culture of satisfied employees, satisfied customers, and successful projects. It is a shame that every stratum of our society does not recognize that we work better when we work together!

Fortunately, my corporate experiences also taught me how to go out and market and sell. I did discover that my business card with my new small-business company's name on it wasn't nearly as valuable as the business card with Monsanto written on it. Now, instead of calling on academics, however, I marketed to clients from a variety of different industries, forming relationships with them as they were renovating existing facilities or adding new buildings to their portfolios. These relationships often resulted in my firm being invited to bid on certain projects as a prequalified invited bidder.

Soon after I started my business, I recognized that my firm was noticeably unique as an African American firm with a PhD-holding leader and that the firm only served commercial clients in a specialized industry, namely horticulture. Initially, there were occasional minor incidents of overt racism, but more often what I dealt with was unintentional racial bias. All of us have biases of one type or another. We acquire them from our families or even sometimes our own experiences in life. Unless they are called out, most of the time we are not even aware that we have them. I began my business during a time of racial and societal change.

Things that my parents experienced as African Americans had been challenged by the Civil Rights Movement and were being addressed. Not everyone likes change. When you are in business you have to learn to work with all kinds of people, and if you maintain a professional persona, most of the time you can win folks over, biases or not. When I would go for a sale with a company, I would let them know I had a PhD in horticulture; I always told them that the PhD was a free bonus. That PhD distinguished me from my competitors. Corporate clients recognized that they were getting a PhD-trained grass cutter or landscaper to develop their property so that they could concentrate on their core business line and still get excellent CURB APPEAL. I learned how to deal with high-level corporate managers, just as I had learned how to deal with high-level academic folk.

Early on during our business start-up years, we landed some great commercial contracts. Some of these are as follows: BMW Automotive was building its first U.S. manufacturing plant in South Carolina, and their German headquarters had plans for upscale landscaping of their fancy high-profile campus. Roche Carolina Pharmaceutical was building a large pharmaceutical plant in the early 1990s with a large acreage and heavily landscaped campus.

Many public-school districts were building new schools to replace those originally built in the 1950s. In addition to installing the original landscaping, most of these clients awarded the long-term daily grounds maintenance contracts to my firm. I was aware that some of these clients were hiring my firm because of the reputation I had made with my knowledge of horticulture. This knowledge enabled them to have an environmentally friendly landscape. It was a bonus also that hiring my firm helped them meet their Equal Employment Opportunity Commission (EEOC) Affirmative Action goals. With a lot of these companies, their strategy was to hire a site work firm, a construction firm, a roofing firm, an electrical firm, a heating and air firm, and a landscape firm. I was a well-trained horticulturist, so I let my clients know that "I'm your curb appeal guy," i.e., the landscape guy with the PhD.

CIVIC INVOLVEMENT IN THE MARKETPLACE

Tomorrow belongs to people who prepare for it today![38]

As God would have it, when Monsanto transferred me to South Carolina, it allowed me to establish a reputation due to my participation in civic activities and public service. The South Carolina General Assembly is responsible for electing board members for the state's publicly funded universities. In 1988, there was a vacancy on the Clemson Board due to the resignation of a member. The SC secretary of agriculture, Les Tindall, encouraged me to apply for the vacancy so that I could help represent the agricultural community as a board member of the state-funded agriculture school. To get elected to the board of a South Carolina publicly funded university, there is a screening process conducted by the State Law Enforcement Agency with stringent background, personal, and financial reviews. So, I took advantage of being the Monsanto guy, also known as the Roundup guy, and ran for the vacant Clemson Board seat. The agricultural community backed my bid to serve on the Clemson Board of Trustees, and I was elected to a four-year term. Since that successful election, I have been the only Black member on the Clemson Board of Trustees. Most of my Board peers are also Clemson alumni and are receptive to my contributions to university governance, especially for the

> **"Tomorrow belongs to people who prepare for it today!"**

agricultural curriculum, research, and county extension services that I have been able to provide.

The Board of Trustees position gave me standing as a civic leader and credibility with the academic community. My credibility with the academic community was due to my being a trustee who had also earned a PhD. They knew I had gone through what most faculty members had gone through to earn their PhD degrees. Historically, most of the trustees of state universities like Clemson are also graduates of the university boards that they serve on. An unintended bonus to this position was that it provided me with many trade and industry connections. The relationships that I developed through Clemson helped me in multiple ways. The area that I lived and worked in provided connections that were quite helpful for me as I grew my business. As I grew my start-up, membership on the Clemson Board allowed me the opportunity to get involved with civic, social, and political issues facing the agricultural community and the Black community. I am not ashamed to let folks know that the Clemson Board of Trustees has given me access to the Captains of Industry and Trade in South Carolina. As of 2020, I have been re-elected to the Clemson Board for nine separate four-year terms.

Another advantage to being on the Board was that when I was given an opportunity to bid on a project, I walked in with not only a PhD but also with the benefit of having been evaluated, investigated, and elected by the South Carolina General Assembly to multiple four-year terms on the Clemson Board of Trustees. The Clemson Board of Trustee elections are held by the General Assembly, so I have often spoken to candidates who were seeking to be elected as judges, or to boards and commissions.

As a business leader, I have been involved in the public square concerning issues impacting the greater good of my local, state, and national communities and marketplace. I have supported candidates who support small business and higher education issues. I have never personally been interested in running for public office; I have always taken the position in my support of elected officials of being a "king maker" and not the king. I have always wanted to see good people in office who are concerned about the needs of the community and also the businesses that operate in that community. It is sage wisdom that the one who helps the king has access to the king when needed.

I take my role as a trustee as an honor as it clearly addresses my desire "to pay forward and to pay back." After first being elected in 1988, I have served as the senior (longest-serving) member of the Clemson Board of Trustees since 2016. I have always taken my trustee role seriously, as I do all the responsibilities that I take on in my life.

What I have given is my time, my talents, and my treasures. Whether it is my role in service to the state or the federal government, civic or local organizations, or professional and social organizations, my philosophy and my mantra is: "PAY YOUR CIVIC RENT, which means that if you're going to eat from the public trough, you must put something back into it." This includes giving credence to the community's political issues, supporting the civic organizations and the philanthropic and nonprofit organizations, and also giving tithes and offerings to my church. My guidance for charitable giving is that I only have a say on the GIVING side of the ledger. The IRS and the Good Lord will take care of the RECEIVING side.

CHAPTER 10

MY PHILOSOPHY ABOUT LIVING THE GOOD LIFE

A Good Life Is Not Only About Doing Well; It Is Also About Doing Good!

Most contemporary philosophers agree that there are as many ways of living a good life as there are people living. Others say, "Life is good when we think it's good, and life is bad when we don't think." In my humble opinion, a good life is a collection of happy moments. From an entrepreneurial perspective, there are three ingredients to the good life: learning, earning, and yearning. Poet Maya Angelou states that "My mission in life is not merely to survive, but to thrive; and to do so with some passion, some compassion, some humor, and some style." Live a good life, and in the end it's not the years in a life, it's the life in the years.

I take nothing for granted. I only have good days and great days. I count life as good as long as I am good. Ambassador Andrew Young said, "I think there is a reason that my parents taught me that life is a burden. But if you take it one day at a time, it's an easy burden." At the end of the day, life is good; or at the very least, it is interesting. The Good Life is also linked to a set of long-term friends who have been with you through the good times and the bad times, typically since childhood. Most of the time, old friends were around as you became the person that you grew up to be. As with family members, old friends are like the wind in your sails. Biblically, the wind is a symbol of the Holy Spirit on the Day of Pentecost (Acts 2:1-2). As a senior citizen, I cherish my old friends. I've accepted that while I often meet new friends and acquaintances, it is rare if not impossible to find or make "new old friends."

The pursuit of God's glory and the pursuit of what is good for us are not two separate pursuits. If you want to do good for people, you must try to reveal God to them. If you want to reveal God and make Him known for who He really is, one way we do this is to make it an aim to do good to others. We must strive to find the kind of balance in our lives where we can devote our lives to doing good and to bringing calm into our own lives and the lives of others. Each person's definition of a good life does not have to look like everyone else's. Whatever aligns your inside with your outside is what you should spend your time doing. While living the GOOD LIFE, we must also continue to fight for justice and defend the weak. And when we help others enjoy the blessings of a good life, we come to fully realize and enjoy the blessings of God in our own life. My life has been good since I dedicated my life to the LORD and found peace of mind. In my daily petitions, I usually pray, "Out of my life, let Jesus shine. Make me a blessing to someone today." I like my life. I have a good life.

The Lord Does Not Just Call the Qualified, He Also Qualifies the Called!

I have also subscribed to the philosophy that in addition to becoming profitable, my business should participate in supporting organizations and missions that serve my local and state communities. I volunteer to serve my community and to help others like I have been helped. I was always taught that, "a leader is one who KNOWS the way, SHOWS the way, and GOES the way."[39.] I recognized when I started my business that, as the leader or the boss, you get the privilege and the opportunity to GO FIRST! I always try to "get a seat at the table" where civic or corporate decisions are made. Personally, at this stage of life, it seems like if you are invited to decision-making meetings and you don't have a seat at the table, "then you are on the menu"! I also adhere to this saying by Theodore Roosevelt: "People don't care how much you know until they know how much you care."

> **"A leader is one who KNOWS the way, SHOWS the way, and GOES the way."**

Recognizing that my business was my platform for Marketplace Ministry was a game-changer for me. I found that my everyday work was the best opportunity to both reach people with my faith and help them reach their dreams. It took some time, but I finally realized I was in the Esther season of my life; I had been positioned *"for such a time as this"* (Esther 4:1).

One of the goals of my life's journey is to make the places where I lived and worked better than they were when I came to them. My major barometer for success became apparent when I saw people gravitating toward me for my advice and counsel. Also, when they came to me because they were attracted to my personal lifestyle or management style. I wanted to help create a community of charity and compassion … to strangers; to the poor; to the homeless; to the needy; to the lonely, sick, and shut in; to the prodigal son and the wayward daughter; to the least, the lost, and the left behind.

My Journey Summarized
Prepare for and Expect Success
*You can live down any number of failures, but
you can't live down a great success.*

When I reflect on the things that have been monumental in my life, there are many. Naturally, my parents were the first ones both to love me and to teach me. My extended family all played a role as well in reinforcing the strong work ethic that my parents adhered to. By the time I entered school, I had a great foundation, which was reinforced by my first teachers, the nuns at my primary school, then the community that consisted of great teachers, strong local and community leaders, and last but certainly not least, my church showing me the path to salvation and living a good life. Ushering me into adulthood, I credit Clemson with both maturing my worldview and shaping my career.

As I grew up, I would often think of the Lord's Prayer, which we were taught as youngsters. I dissected parts of it so I could see how it applied to me. As I saw other youngsters trying to be grown up and tough guys, they would curse and use the Lord's Name in vain. If we were having lunch with a group, I always stopped the group, a practice I continue even today, to say a blessing. It goes back to the scripture that says if you're ashamed of the Lord, He's going to be ashamed of you. I see that the most monumental theme on my life's journey has been to seek God, honor God, and obey God.

This brings me to the numerous references to journeys in the scriptures. From the exodus of the Israelites from Egypt in the Old Testament to the day the saints will be taken up to be with the Lord in the New Testament. A strong part of my life journey has centered on work. In the book of Ecclesiastes, the preacher writes, "*Whatever your hand finds to do, verily do it with all your might*" (Ecclesiastes 9:10). Individual goals are set and achieved through hard work, rarely by chance. Those who accomplish great things pay attention to little things. Individual goals can even be achieved by happenstance, e.g., you wake up one morning and you've reached a goal that you didn't work for, but it is a worthwhile goal, nonetheless. That success not only benefits you individually, but it benefits the people around you, or even society in general. The level of success is determined by how success leads to contributing to local, state, national, or even global actions.

After seminary, I adopted my life's verse as a mission statement for my company. It is: *"And we know that all things work together for good to them that love God, to them who are called according to His purpose"* (Romans 8:28). It's a blessing to be a blessing. My contribution to the greater good of my community begins and ends with me. Biblically, you could think of success as a blessing: a blessing to you, a blessing to others, contributing to the greater good of me, or contributing to the greater good of society. These goals can be biblically reconciled through scripture as Jesus stated, *"Let your light shine before others, so that they may see your good works and give glory to your Father who is in heaven"* (Matthew 5:16).

Believers and nonbelievers alike know that fame and fortune can be fleeting. Psalm 49:17 gives biblical meaning to this adage. This scripture reminds us that rich and poor alike should remember that money is temporary. It is not a substitute for God's approval. All people face death and God's judgment. There is no reason to envy a person who has earthly wealth but lacks eternal hope. In my daily prayers, I typically end with: "Lord, out of my life, let Jesus shine; make me a blessing to someone each day." Delivering that blessing is success, and receiving a God-given blessing is a success. My goal in business and in life is to make the world a better place than it was before I came. To significantly contribute to the Greater Good. Blessed are those who give without remembering and take without forgetting.

> **"Blessed are those who give without remembering and take without forgetting."**

Adages From My Life

- Don't count the days, make the days count. (Muhammed Ali)
- You don't get a second chance to make a first impression. (Will Rogers, Oscar Wilde)
- Don't insult the alligator until after you have crossed the lagoon. (Southern folk saying)
- Sometimes you're the windshield; sometimes you're the bug. (Sung by Mary Chapin Carpenter; Producers: John Jennings, Mary Chapin Carpenter, and Steve Buckingham, 1992.)
- A man who carries a cat by the tail learns something that he can learn no other way. (Mark Twain)
- Good judgment comes from experience, and a lot of that comes from bad judgment. (Will Rogers)
- Sometimes you get, and sometimes you get got. (John Wooden)
- The truth doesn't hurt unless it ought to. (B. C. Forbes)
- Make peace with your past so it won't screw up the present. (Multiple authors)
- It doesn't take a very big person to carry a grudge. (Proverb)
- What other people think of you is none of your business. (Deepak Chopra, Regina Brett)
- No one ever drowned in sweat. (U.S. Drill Instructor)
- Character is a journey, not a destination. (Bill Clinton)

- Character is much easier kept than recovered. (Thomas Paine)

- Character is what you have left when you've lost everything that you can lose. (Evan Eser)

- If a relationship has to be secret, you shouldn't be in it. (Regina Brett)

- Some people leave a mark, others leave a stain. (Eleanor Roosevelt)

- The cheese in a mousetrap is free. (Stephen Covey)

- A remark generally hurts or offends in proportion to its truth to the listener. (Will Rogers)

- Dealing with the seasons of your life. (Eleanor Roosevelt and Bill Keane are usually credited with this phrase for use of this quote in the caption under The Family Circus newspaper cartoon from 8/31/1994.)

  ○ Yesterday is history.

  ○ Tomorrow is a mystery.

  ○ Tomorrow is a gift – that is why we call it the present.

- Fortune befriends the bold. (Latin Proverb: Virgil)

- Opportunity knocks, but it is never a long-time visitor in one's life. (Modern Adage)

- There are no secrets to success. It is the result of preparation, hard work, and learning from failure. (Colin Powell)

- Every skill you acquire doubles your odds of success. (Scott Adams)

MY LEADERS

CHAPTER 11

WHAT IS LEADERSHIP TO ME?

It's Not All Motherhood and Apple Pie.

Leadership is the ability of an individual or a group of people to influence and guide followers to do what they expect in terms of performance for that organization, society, or team. My guidance for aspiring leaders is, "Don't follow the crowd; let the crowd follow you."[40] Leadership is often an attribute tied to a person's title, seniority, or ranking in a hierarchy. There are many ways to execute the authority that comes from leadership. With leadership comes authority and power. The execution of power can range from trying to force people to do something against their will or to doing something as simple as providing and disseminating information to a group that you hope will adhere to that information. Legitimate or official power oversees a group with the expectation that they will follow those directives as a response to the leader's position. Many leaders deliver a kind of exchanged or rewarded power, whereby they let the people they are leading know that they have an agreement with them—the employee "doing this," and then they will in return "get that." When there is a level of respect for a leader based upon the leader's personality, or their relationship with higher ups, or with their proven record of success, this is called referent power. Finally, expert power flows from an individual that uses their knowledge or expertise over an area or over individuals that they are responsible for managing.

I have seen and experienced many kinds of leadership. Even as a child on the playgrounds there was leadership. One child or group of children would exercise dominance over the rest of the children. Over the years and with the changing times, I saw an exhibition of leadership styles from watching television entertainment shows and television news. Whether it was entertainment or the evening news, there was always one who rose in significance over others, exerting a kind of authority over the group. There was also that kind of leadership that made me grimace as I saw reports of gang and riot leadership. I learned the kind of leadership styles that exist among "motherhood and apple pie organizations" like the Boy Scouts and the 4-H Club. This could be witnessed both in the ranks of the leaders and in the community of the members. Then, there were the organizational leadership styles I experienced as a member of the high school marching band and with my college marching band. Sometimes leadership positions were assigned; other times they were assumed by those who were able to lead their peers and motivate them to achieve desired goals. During my college ROTC days and after being commissioned as an army lieutenant, I learned about military leadership, which usually came from earned rank. In my leisure time, I have had a front seat to sports leadership both on and off the field. In the marketplace, I witnessed many styles of political and civic leadership, sometimes with the most unlikely rising to leadership positions. There is no doubt that I not only witnessed church leadership but was also able to be trained in it during my seminary study of Marketplace Ministry. When it was time for me to step into my business as a leader, I was determined to look at the different kinds of leadership traits and decide which of those traits I would ascribe to, which ones fit my personality, my moral compass, and my spiritual beliefs.

Intuitively, I knew that the first leaders in my life had been my parents. There are only two lasting bequests that we can give our children; one of these is ROOTS, and the other is WINGS. My parents gave me both roots and wings. My roots were entrenched in the knowledge and behavior that became the foundation of my character and faith. My wings are the knowledge and the courage that they instilled in me to practice that character and faith in all kinds of places and situations. They led me from birth until I became a responsible adult. They set the foundation and guardrails for my belief system. As I matured, it was the leaders and influencers in my life who proved to me that "iron sharpens iron." The beliefs of my leaders were instilled in me to such an extent that they became the core of my own beliefs and subsequently my leadership style. I developed and honed my leadership style to include metrics that included accomplishment of goals, organizational efficiency, and ultimately profitability as a measure and reflection of the quality of leadership that I was exhibiting and practicing. After applying those metrics to my company's performance, I determined whether to continue using my identified practices or to refine my leadership practices to achieve performance.

On the playground, I saw a view of the kind of leadership that is based on the attitude of the followers. The playground was the first safe place I unknowingly practiced leadership. A natural progression of opportunities was presented for me to view leadership, as well as the opportunity of becoming a leader through the clubs and organizations that I was a part of, such as 4-H Clubs, Boy Scouts, the marching band, the NAACP, and the National Urban League. It was in these organizations that I was able to closely observe various levels of leading as well as coming into my own conscious leadership. Leadership is about more than telling people what to do or where to go. Leadership not only directs but also inspires people to be all that they can be. This has been my experience with the leaders in my life. Beginning with my own grandfathers and father who not only told me about life's lessons but exemplified what they taught through their own lives.

I reflected on my journey of life to identify, learn, and adopt a leadership style that fit me best. From childhood until starting my professional career, I observed the styles of civic, political, sports, church, academic, and social leaders. I tried to determine which one fit me best. In the final analysis, I determined that my management and leadership style extracts elements of sports leadership, military leadership, church leadership, academic leadership, and leadership in the marketplace.

SPORTS LEADERSHIP

Over many years, I identified the type of leadership that existed in sports. There is evidence of distinct levels, such as the coach vs. the quarterback. In sports, we find multiple levels of leadership, which must interact at the same time. Australian politician and coach Ric Charlesworth said, "The interesting thing about coaching is that you have to trouble the comfortable and comfort the troubled." There are times when "sports style" leadership applies to organizations. A relatively new cottage industry has developed the team leadership style that has evolved over the years and is called "executive leadership coaching," where members of organizations refer to each other as teammates.

> **"In coaching you sometimes you have to trouble the comfortable and sometime you have to comfort the troubled"**

MILITARY LEADERSHIP

With my experience in the military, it was not difficult to determine that each rank has its duties, responsibilities, and privileges, for the military makes these leadership role distinctions very clear. Military academies teach aspiring officers that the only battle we fight for is the trust and affection of our men—they win the rest. General Douglas MacArthur said, "A true leader has the confidence to stand alone, the courage to make tough decisions, and the compassion to listen to the needs of others. He does not set out to be a leader but becomes one by the equality of his actions and the integrity of his intent."

CHURCH LEADERSHIP

In my opinion, Christian leadership is a call to serve as clergy or lay leaders. In the religious community, leaders provide a moral barometer that includes seeking God in making decisions concerning their leadership. Leaders are God's gift to mankind. "Servant leadership" is a term often used to describe how Jesus led—as a servant to His followers. The question arises, are "servant leadership" and "Christ-centered leadership" one and the same? The servant leader is a servant first. The Christ-centered leader is both a servant and one who intentionally waits on God for direction. I accept church leadership as the voice that directs and channels spiritual and civic behavior in the capacity of both a leader and a follower. From studying the Bible, I reached the conclusion that God created leaders for all tribes, tongues, genders, and ages.

ACADEMIC LEADERSHIP

Going into the world of academia, I saw a different kind of leadership. There were those who advised me, those who taught me, and those who made decisions about the quality of my performance compared to their expectations as measured by tasks completed or presentation in the form of projects. Society recognizes that the key to being a good student is a great school, and the key to a great school is a great principal. All of us have memories and stories about the leadership of good teachers in our lives. Having raised three children with a strong belief in academics, I know that good classroom leaders contribute to shaping children. I have a number of teachers in my family, and I see how they share child-raising tasks with parents. I say that classroom and school leaders are the only people who lose sleep over other people's children.

MARKETPLACE LEADERSHIP

When I started my career in the corporate world, I understood leadership in a whole new way. A major goal of leadership in the marketplace is to monetize the labor, professional services, products, or relationships of the workforce. In the marketplace, employees learn to perform tasks directed by people who of necessity take credit or blame for the outcomes of their work. On the many boards and commissions that I have served on, I learned that the board develops organizational goals that are overseen by business line executives. The line manager's task is to report to business line executives, who communicate, advocate, and direct the accomplishment of board goals.

In my worldview, no matter what the style, leaders honor and submit to God's authority. From Genesis to Revelation, the Bible highlights leaders who honored God by loving Him and doing what He requested of those who made a decision to choose to bring glory to God and honor to themselves. I attended seminary to study Marketplace Ministry to develop my leadership style to match what I believe was God's will for my life.

LEADER LESSONS

Every great leader is a great teacher, and the greatest leaders seize every opportunity to teach well. [41]

"**Every great leader is a great teacher, and the greatest leaders seize every opportunity to teach well.**"

As I progressed through grade school and college, more leaders were added to my life. My teachers were important in formulating and encouraging my belief in myself and my ability to do well. Pastors and civic leaders became additional leaders whose opinions influenced my understanding and decisions about what is right and wrong. As the Black leaders in my community became united, they would meet to see what young people could advance the cause of Civil Rights, particularly with the integration of schools. It was these leaders who worked with my parents and determined that it would be in my best interest to attend Clemson. This experience gave me exposure to civic leadership for the greater good of a community or a people group.

The Clemson academic experience is a good example of how God gifts individuals and people with a designated journey and destination. Man is always just one decision from journeying outside of God's design. When we take steps away from God's design, we face an uncertain future. Our destination becomes unclear. When that destination is unclear, so is our journey. Clemson was my first faith test away from Mama and Daddy. My church away from home was Abel Baptist Church, a legacy

Black church in Clemson. That church welcomed students and members and also provided advice, counsel, and support just like I received at home.

I believe that the influence of a good teacher can never be erased. It is said that teachers affect eternity since they never know where their influence ends. The church has that mantra as well. I have many business associates who are serving their community and their fellow man, exhibiting the principles they learned at church. I was blessed to have many teachers who were concerned about "if" and "how" I mastered subjects. It is my belief that good teachers don't work just for income, but more for outcome. It has been my experience that good teachers never strive to explain their vision. They simply invite you to stand beside them and see it yourself. In the current landscape of the types and size of various schools, it is evident that you can pay educational leaders and administrators to teach, but you cannot pay them to care. As a long-serving 35+ year member of higher education boards and commissions, my challenge to the academic community is that "to educate a man in mind only and not in morals also is but to educate a menace to society."[42]

> "To educate a man in mind only and not in morals also is but to educate a menace to society."

CHAPTER 12

WHO I AM AS A LEADER

WHAT KIND OF LEADER HAVE I BEEN TO MY EMPLOYEES?

I've concluded that the metric by which my life will be assessed won't be in dollars, but by the individual people whose lives I've touched.[43]

One of the things I noticed from observing the businesses in my family is that they had loyal employees who were like family, and those employees worked hard for the business. The employees saw that their families were being provided for, and they never had to worry about their paychecks. Through my business, I am often used to deliver a job, a paycheck, a word of encouragement, or a blessing to others. I have also learned that what Maya Angelou said is true: "People will forget what you said, people will forget what you did, but people will never forget how you made them feel."

My Leadership Guiding Principles

My philosophy in my business was and is one that I inherited from my parents and grandparents. The employees get paid first, before I get paid. My goal has been and will always be to adhere to that, and I can say, my company has never missed a payroll. I always told my employees that if I did good,

"Management is doing things right, while leadership is doing the right thing."

they would do good. "Management is doing things right, while leadership is doing the right thing."[44] I wanted to not only reap the benefits of my hard work but to see that my employees did also. I also saw that giving people a little more than they expect is a good way to get a lot more than you expect as implied in scripture (Luke 12:48). My personnel management style adheres to the tenet of an old saying: "To handle yourself, use your head; to handle others, use your heart."[45] During personnel management sessions, I work at keeping my words soft and sweet due to the current litigious workplace attitudes, since you never know if you'll have to eat your words. We all know that the bitterest words are those that we are forced to eat. My approach is supported by an old saying by farmers: "Don't wrestle with a pig. It gets you muddy, and the pig actually enjoys it!" There were practices I witnessed when watching my father and my uncle conduct their business. Paying attention to their setting a business tone yet maintaining a certain and supportive work environment was a good model for me to build upon. It worked for my Dad, and it has worked for me.

Since starting my business, it has been very important to me that my employees know that I am a man of good character. I understand that for individuals, character is destiny, and for organizations, culture is destiny. Adhering to the wisdom of Eleanor Roosevelt, I subconsciously classified the job skills of candidates into one of three categories:

1. People who make things happen

2. People who watch things happen

3. People who wonder what happened[46]

My Leadership Control Style
I Do Not Mind a Mistake, But I
Do Mind the Same Mistake

It is not mistakes that define who we are; it is how we recover from those mistakes.[47]

Success does not consist of never making mistakes but in never making the same mistake a second time. I encourage and remind employees that experience tells you what to do and confidence allows you to do it. I often remind and advise mentees that you don't get a second chance to make a first impression. I sometimes choose a lazy person to do a hard job because a lazy person will find an easy way to do it. Years ago, I gave up on trying to make tasks "fool proof," for I have come to realize that fools are so clever that they can figure out what I'm trying to do! I have often counseled inexperienced but enthusiastic employees about the traps of multitasking while learning new tasks. For some folks, multitasking turns out to be doing several things poorly at the same time. When assigning or evaluating employees, my father's decisions kept in mind the proverb, "Even a blind squirrel will find an acorn every now and then," and for a practical comparison, remember that "even a broken clock is right twice a day."[48]

In many instances, multitasking turns out to be the art of simultaneously doing several things badly. I despise and discourage busyness. We all know that time spent is not necessarily an indicator of success. In my opinion, busyness is moral laziness because it does not require individuals to live or act with courage since courageous acts are intentional. "Courage is fear that has said its prayers!"[49] As a leader, it is important to give your team credit. I praise loudly; I blame softly. I am in full agreement with the now popular saying, "Teamwork makes the dream work."[50]

What worked for me was not telling people how to do things but telling them what to do and then letting them surprise me with their results. The spiritual aspect of my leadership style is to be humble and to be thankful and grateful for the position that I am in. Old folks used to repeat a proverb, "If you fall off a horse, dust yourself off and get back on and try again." When failures occur, I tell folks there's something to be learned from every failure. An important lesson that I've abided by was to extract a "lesson learned" from failed tasks, especially the ones that caused physical harm or ego damage. There is another proverb that says, "A burnt child fears fire"; therefore, I am particularly careful to avoid situations that might lead to that same mistake, like touching a hot stove top.

However, sometimes after repeated failures of the same task, I say to poor performers, "How long have you been working here, not counting tomorrow?"[51] When counseling or discipling employees, I take compassionate but appropriate actions. It is said that a wise man's questions contain half the answer. One of my mentors told me to do as physicians do, treat the cold not the cough. My advice to others is that it is not how we make mistakes; it's how we correct them. Leaders must anticipate that they will have some unwilling followers who openly or indiscreetly cause nonacceptance or at least push back against proposed tasks. In these situations, we have to deal with them one on one.

LEADERSHIP: LEARNING MY STYLE
Before you are a leader, success is about growing yourself
When you become a leader, success is about growing others[52]

In many cases, whatever job that I oversaw, at one time or another I had been the one following someone else's leadership in doing that job. I witnessed different leadership styles, particularly noticing that some of them were negative. Conversely, I saw others in leadership who were extremely positive and created an atmosphere that worked very well.

I wanted to make sure that I was approachable and easy to talk to as an employer. I tactfully embraced this style, but I always jokingly reminded employees that I may have been born at night, but not last night—I didn't just fall off the back of a turnip truck. I was surprised when I noticed that all employees aren't necessarily motivated by money alone; some are more motivated by pride and recognition. Early in my career as a leader and manager, I quickly learned that you do not lead by hitting people over the head. So, I added a metric of encouragement that I call "the carrot and the stick." The "stick" figuratively represents the punishment, and the "carrot" represents the reward. I made it so that to get to the carrot required extra effort. I also made sure that the "stick" would not be so intimidating that people were afraid to take a chance.

As I matured, I assumed a role of humility, which worked for my elders and was already a part of my personality. Instead of viewing humility as a measure of reduced confidence, I discovered what Norman Peale said, "People with humility don't think less of themselves, they just think of themselves less." One thing that I've learned over the years is that the major occupational hazard to good leadership is pride. As a boss, it is nice to be important, but it is more important to be nice. From the beginning, I worked at being a beloved boss rather than a hated boss by being fair and not hurting employees' feelings. In any organization, you are going to find people who may not approve of the way that you do things, for whatever reason. These are commonly referred to as "haters." While it's not my style, I know some associates who have found success and personal satisfaction through finding a pathway to live in the heads of their haters. I have learned that hurt is worse than anger since anger that dwells in the head can fade. Hurt lingers in the soul and rarely if ever fades. Isn't it funny that people who know the least about you have the most to say about you?

My leadership style evolved into a collaborative approach, emphasizing partnership. I have always tried to exude a respect for the ability of my employees. I'd give the person something to do, and I'd encourage them to do it and give them help only if needed. I also discovered that if the task was beyond their skill set, I should not beat them up and put them down but give them advice on how to do it better or remove them from the task without destroying their confidence. In my organization, I worked hard to eliminate the "just a" syndrome, where lower-level employees would say, "I cannot do this or that because I am 'just a' secretary, or grass cutter, or janitor." We don't hire any "just a" employees. Today our management culture has embraced the belief that all employees at all levels are called TEAMMATES.

For Who Knows That the Lord Placed You in This Time or Place for "Such a Time as This"

"If your actions inspire others to dream more, learn more, do more and become more, you are a leader."[53]

In this life, we are all living out a particular role. Some of us are leaders, and some of us are content to be followers. Being a follower is just as important as being a leader; you can't have one without the other. Roles change over the years, as someone can be a follower today and a leader tomorrow. In addition, you can be a leader in your job and a follower someplace else, like at church.

I have come to identify where I am at this time in my life. While reading the Biblical Book of Esther, I saw that my life now can be described as, *"for such a time as this"* (Esther 4:4). I know that my decisions, my behavior, and my performance have an effect not only on me but on other people as well. I continue to strive to see that my performance as a business leader provides what is in the best interest of not only my family but my employees and my community as well.

Leaders must be willing and able to take "positions." As a business leader, I am still learning that it takes courage to stand up and speak, and it also takes courage to sit down and listen. No matter which aspect of life we are dealing in, especially in business it is true that "Fools often live to regret their words, and wise men sometimes live to regret their silence."

> **"Fools often live to regret their words, and wise men sometimes live to regret their silence."**

My favorite guidance by a mentor is a story told to me about knowing when to shut up. They told the story like this: "If you find yourself in a hole, stop digging. After chasing a herd of cattle, then catching, killing, and eating an entire bull, a mountain lion felt so good he started roaring. He kept it up until a hunter came along, saw the dead bull's carcass, and shot him. The moral: When you're full of bull, keep your mouth shut![54]

Some leaders are just the showboat sitting in the captain's chair. A fitting axiom for that type of leadership can be found in sailor tales: "A ship in harbor is safe, but that is not what ships are for."[55] You'll never hear anyone say, "And then they all gave up." A Greek proverb by Alexander the Great states, "An army of sheep led by a lion will always defeat an army of lions led by a sheep."[56]

It has often been said that whatever you are doing, perform that task to the best of your ability, and then you will get rewarded. Sometimes the reward is just a mental uplift; sometimes it involves ego awards. As I matured in the business, I would often tell my employers, "If you do good, I do good. If I do good, you do good. So, let's partner and make this thing work." I saw this approach worked, and I continue to use it today. It is so true that "past performance is the best predictor of future performance." Past performance builds confidence and trust with new customers. Yet as I've gotten older, I'm even more willing to help folks who work directly for me or folks that I'm mentoring to see that their future performance is always better. I accept and adopt the advice that there are three major things needed to be successful: a backbone, a wishbone, and a funny bone.[57] I explain this as follows: a backbone signifies the time and effort required to be successful, i.e., sweat equity; a wishbone allows one to accept and recognize the value of being in the right place at the right time, i.e., divine intervention; and a funny bone allows one to be able to laugh at setbacks then learn from mistakes or obstacles by getting up and trying again.

My Leadership
Comparison With My Dad's Leadership
"My father gave me the greatest gift anyone could give another person: He believed in me."[58]

There is no doubt I have a business entrepreneurial gene in me, and that gene has been passed down and continues to operate in my family. My children now appear to have that gene, as they now have their own businesses. What I learned from my Dad and my uncles from the meat business that influenced me the most was the collaboration and partnership that existed between them.

Both my Uncle Marvin and my Dad wanted me to be a veterinarian, but I loved plants and especially growing plants. I decided to study horticulture, and in the 1960s and 1970s as I was determining what career I wanted to go for, there was a group who were referred to as members of the Flower Child movement. I can remember my Dad jokingly saying, "Son I'm proud of you, but I've got a meat packing plant, and you are a professional Flower Child." When I got a job with a national agrichemical firm working on products like the popular weed killer Roundup, Dad began to see how my vocation was paying off. Prior to his death, he closed the butcher shop, and his retirement hobby was growing flowers, particularly sunflowers. You can say that Daddy became a Flower Child too!

Looking back, even in high school, I joined clubs and organizations that taught me trade practices and business philosophies. I was in the 4-H Club, and I had projects raising animals and growing vegetable gardens. I was in the Boy Scouts where I helped organize and participated in projects to help my local community or those in need within my community. I made it a practice to reach out and do projects that benefited the community. Early on, I wanted to learn about the many aspects of a business. I knew that If I was going to be a good businessman, I would have to be prepared academically to be a leader and to think logically as a businessperson. I knew I needed to understand finances, local economics, and even global economics. I worked hard to learn these things. The more education I got, the more I knew I needed, to be prepared in and to focus on a certain niche. I knew I needed a unique set of skills that could be translated into meeting a need that was marketable. I liked gardening and I grew up on a farm. I decided that I would go into horticulture. I did not want to just have a cursory view of horticulture; I wanted to know all the trade secrets and have the academic credentials to prove it.

Based on the leaders that I saw and worked with in 4-H Club, I aspired to be a county agent. I knew that if I was going to be a county agent, I would need a college degree from an agricultural college. I remember as a youngster an instance when my Dad was growing crops of cabbage that had been infested with whiteflies. My Dad got the local county agent to come out, and he told him how to get rid of that insect. The county agent also told him what he could do to prevent insects, diseases, and weeds in his crops. My Dad made a decent living from his butcher shop and vegetable crops with the advice and counsel of agricultural specialists. I reasoned in my mind that I could be a farmer, but I could also help many farmers as a county agent. As an elementary student, I didn't realize at the time that I could also be a high school ag teacher or a college professor. My vision did not stretch that far. What I did know was that I wanted to be an advisor to both myself and to others as to how to improve their production practices and ultimate profitability.

Being my own boss meant that I had to be the leader, and I had to learn some lessons about leadership. While working in Corporate America, I always had a boss, and that boss, in their leadership role, told me what to do and sometimes told me how to do it. When I started my business, I developed a commitment that being the boss meant that I had to go first and lead by example. From my time in the military, I saw that one of the practices of good leaders was to lead by example. After a few months in the business where I was the boss, I saw that there were many things about good leadership traits that I needed to learn and apply. I did a study of different types of leadership styles to determine what type of leader was most fitting for me. From a personal perspective, I learned that "you can take a day off, but you can't take it back."

When I arrived at the stage of my life where I was making career decisions, I knew I did not want to be a follower. I knew that service does not so much establish your choice as confirm your choice. Onlookers can see what you are choosing, but they can't quickly comprehend what and whom you serve. God is glorified when believers live like believers. Each day I strive that out of my life Jesus will shine … and that I will be a blessing to someone each day. When I became an entrepreneur after almost two decades in Corporate America, I started a business that is now almost 40 years old.

If I were to speak as to what the key to my success as a businessman is, the first thing I would have to attest to is that

I surrounded myself with people who were smarter than me. I question why some managers hire extremely smart people and then tell them what to do. It has been my approach to hire smart people and let them tell me what to do. I say to other business owners that the first prerequisite to a functioning business is to know you must work hard and to have competent staff who understand that as well. The second component is equally important, having access to sufficient capital. Being aligned to other small-business programs locally and nationally is a key component as well.

CHAPTER 13

WHAT I DISCOVERED ABOUT SUCCESS FROM MY LEADERS

I soon learned that life and business are tough teachers in that "they give the test first then the lesson."[59] H. Jackson Brown in his work *Life's Little Instruction Book* states that the only place where success occurs before work is in the dictionary. There is no doubt in my mind that there are many who have contributed to my success. First of course are my parents, the ones who raised me. They instilled in me values and business acumen by the things they did and the things they required and encouraged me to do. They defined what success looked like for me, and their wisdom has followed me all my life. That same kind of guidance and direction came from my extended family, including my grandfathers and my uncles. Their personal success was both in terms of influence and affluence. The building blocks for my success belong to the people that educated me from kindergarten through to my obtaining my PhD.

I have learned not to be afraid to ask for help. It is important to remember that help is best defined by the recipient, not the bestower. There are some other wise things I learned from mentors. I have used them to navigate my business dealings with both clients and employees. One of the main things I have come to understand is that the basis of any relationship, particularly a business relationship, is trust. It soon becomes evident in a working relationship that trust and character don't show up on a balance sheet.

WORK Through CONTRACTS

If you can trust a man ... then a written
contract is a waste of paper.
If you can't trust a man, then a written
contract is still a waste of paper.[60]

When establishing a business relationship, the first determinant has to be how you begin that relationship. In order to have a profitable end, it is essential to make certain assessments. If you fail to make a good assessment, your business relationship could be both time-consuming and costly. Over the years I've had many partners, and I learned it is good practice to never choose a partner whose values are different from yours. The common-sense logic of this policy is that it does not pay to fight a skunk because even if you win, you lose. There must be some fundamental agreements based upon shared beliefs established at the beginning. The contract needs to clarify the responsibilities of both parties, and it must be mutually agreed upon. The best contract is prepared where both parties can see each other eye to eye and face to face. You can learn a lot about a person by observing their body language.

There must be agreed-on points of assessment to determine if both parties are living up to the aforestated terms. One thing is certain, "communication and trust generally fall at the same time." When adequate measures are not met at ascertained times, one or the other of the parties are going to feel as if they are not getting adequate service or respect. Thus, a contract with clear, concise, and mutually agreed upon terms, with clearly stated points of assessment, is most profitable in the long run. Based on his experience as a sharecropper, my Dad always reminded me to keep an eye on the books. I have adopted Dad's "cash flow" management principle in partnerships, remembering something that Mark Twain said: "Figures don't Lie, but liars do figure."

READ and Follow the CONTRACT

A good experience is what you get when you read the fine print, and a bad experience is what you get when you don't read the fine print.[61]

> **"A good experience is what you get when you read the fine print, and a bad experience is what you get when you don't read the fine print."**

In all aspects of my life, I have learned and suffered from the fact that the author of a contract typically often writes it in their favor unless challenged. When purchasing homes or cars, I've learned to carefully read terms and have often been able to get them modified or removed. Especially when entering construction contracts, I have had owners and architects who included unrealistic completion dates, requirements that were different from design documents, undefined owner requirements, and unrealistic warranty items. When the fine print involved price disputes, I relied on my Dad's saying to customers, which is: "Customer, you know that you can't be the buyer and the seller too." When I reduce prices, I make sure that the customer knows that I'm making a comparable reduction in services. If I make too much of a price concession, then it could appear that I was initially overcharging. Always tell the TRUTH to your clients. That way you don't have to remember what you said in the past.

WHERE DID I GAIN MY BUSINESS INSIGHT?

I have made it no secret that I always glean from those who are wiser than I am. My teachers and mentors afforded me an accepted place in a learned society. They also provided me with experiences that enabled me to benefit from business skills financially. My academic leaders taught me how to think logically and how to logically think. This has been perhaps one of the most beneficial things that I acquired. It is a must for a businessman, as someone who relies on their emotions rather than logic can hurt the business. I cannot diminish the importance of recognizing that learning my ABCs well enough to pass standardized tests enabled me to get into college, and that hard work and perseverance enabled me to perform well so I could stay in college. I also had sound direction as to what I wanted to study, which also helped. My teachers made sure that I didn't lose track of who I was and led me not to settle for less than my best. And of course, I always had the church to remind me of "who" I was and "whose" I was. It certainly helped knowing that God was there to guide me along the way.

The money you can make is not the only thing that is important. Most people fail to realize that money is both a test and a trust from God. Having money does not change you ... it just amplifies who you are: jerks become bigger jerks ... and ... nice guys become nicer.

> **"Having money does not change you ... it just amplifies who you are"**

Having reliable, trustworthy mentors who were available to keep me grounded with their sage wisdom was a gift. Yet if I had not heeded their wisdom and knowledge, it would not have profited me anything. Mentors are the people who enhanced my academic knowledge with practical common-sense knowledge. They taught me skills that allowed me to be successful. They also taught me about some of the pitfalls of business.

"Wise men talk when they have something to say, and fools talk because they have to say something."

Having an idea for a business is not enough; even having a good business plan is not enough. In order to be successful in business, there is a need to enlist the wisdom of someone who has been down the road you want to go, for experience is the best teacher of all. When mentees feel as if they have everything so solid, that nothing can go wrong, they are usually on a path that will end up not being productive. When I find myself in an advisory mentoring role, I utilize my own homegrown way of evaluating my mentee: "Wise men talk when they have something to say, and fools talk because they have to say something."[62]

I have noticed that good mentors have mastered the skill of lifting others while they are climbing. When I became a senior citizen, I kept my mentoring skills sharp by sharing experiences and opinions with other successful senior citizens. These sessions of senior citizens exchanging information were often held over informal and sometimes scheduled breakfast or lunch meetings. We easily fit the description of ROMEOS, which is a loosely linked group, across this nation, mostly informal but like-minded RETIRED OLD MEN EATING OUT!

Advice may not always be in terms of their business strategies; a mentor or coach can see you failing to adequately establish proper boundaries with your personal life. It is when someone fails to take heed of sound advice regarding family and/or the amount of time and attention that they give to their family that they may find themselves shipwrecked. Family troubles have a strange way of creeping into your ability to effectively manage your business. As I have grown older, I pay less attention to what men say. I just watch what they do.

CHAPTER 14

THE PRACTICE OF LEADERSHIP

Reach One, Teach One.[63]

A mentor is an experienced and trusted advisor. Mentors offer a safe space for mentees to share concerns, seek guidance, and receive honest feedback. Mentors also connect mentees with people and perspectives that they can use to advance their career. Having a mentor who can teach you the nuances of what you are trying to accomplish is a treasure. A good mentor lifts you up to another level, giving you a hand up, not a handout. They are someone you can share private things with, discuss them, and know that they are not going to share those things you talked about with anyone else. They go beyond textbook knowledge to give you a "been there, done that" experience, which can prevent you from having to go through the same thing or making the same mistakes. I tell my employees that I don't mind mistakes; I just have a problem with making the same mistakes. For me, mistakes are lessons I can learn from that will help me to never do that same thing again. Unexpected things happen more often than we like. However, after the unexpected happens, why is it that there is always someone who claims to have known that it would happen?

Having several good mentors was one of the most important contributors to my business success. I found and clung to mentors from my developmental years, my academic life, my religious life, my civic life, and my social life who encouraged me and helped me find mentors in the industry and trade that I worked in. These were folks who saw something in me, in both the corporate world and in my own business, and who poured into me with their caring and knowledge. One thing that I assured my mentors was that I would not disappoint them. Your word is your bond as much today as it has ever been. For my mentor's help, I returned their effort with an attitude of gratitude. I expressed my gratitude to them by giving of my time, my talent, and my treasure. I want to be the same person in business as I am at home and in church. I advise young career builders that they should not lie to their trusted advisors, since no man has a good enough memory to be a successful liar.

When you make a practice of always telling the truth, you never have to guess about what you said; it's always just the truth every time. I'm that guy who is always disappointed when a liar's pants don't catch on fire!

Mentoring
"Get One, Be One"

Usually, mentors are people who have achieved a good deal of success, or they are old guys who have been around a long time. It is helpful for folks to seek advice from people who have attained a level of success. For the mentee to be successful, I say, "to be one, they've got to see one." I've been on both sides of the spectrum. When people come to me and ask that I mentor them, I consider it an honor. As a mentor you make it possible for your mentees to benefit from some of the things you benefited from. I remind them that there is a difference between giving a hand and giving a handout! Mentees are now standing on your shoulders; however, I tell my mentees that someday they will have to be the shoulders some folks stand on.

"A fool convinced against his will is of the same opinion still."

I quickly evaluate the mindset of the folks who I mentor to determine their level of business preparation, management skills, and personal savvy. I have learned over the years that "a fool convinced against his will is of the same opinion still." Therefore, I avoid mentees who are overly arrogant or clearly ignorant about their business pursuits. An intelligent person recognizes their limitations; those who are unteachable usually do not think they have any limitations. I will always attempt to give a person who comes to me advice, but if I see that they are not receptive, I don't waste their time or mine.

I strongly encourage mentees to pay it forward. My generation and those just behind me, we're all in the paying-back phase of our lives from those things we benefited from. I have benefited from a lot of government programs. My company has constructed a number of buildings and roads on military bases around the Southeast. My philosophy regarding this is that if you are going to feed from the public trough (i.e., government contracts), you must put something back in it. If you are in business, especially if you have government customers, then you have a duty to "pay your civic rent" and give back.

Let me break that down. If you feed from the public trough, then you are obligated to put something back in it. Specifically, on giving back, choose the issue or organization you want to support and then give of your TIME and your TALENT and your TREASURES. Also, only be concerned about the giving side of the ledger. The Good Lord and the IRS will take care of the receiving side!

Trusted Advisors
Honor and Do Not Forget About the Folks Who Were With You on Your Way Up.

The people who were the most valuable to me were those in my hometown. Of additional benefit were the friends and relationships that I developed over the years while in the different cities I worked in while in Corporate America. Yet, it was the place where people who knew me best, the ones who knew me before I was educated, the ones whose efforts paved the way for me to be educated and put me in a position to achieve success; these I honor. So, home sweet home has been good to me. Being in the right place at the right time falls under the adage of the biblical verse that, *"the Lord was ordering my steps." (Psalm 119:133). Look at God!*

THE MAN OF GOD WITH A WORD FROM GOD

There were also preachers in my life. As I moved from city to city, I met a lot of preachers and sat under the teachings of a lot of good preachers and deacons. In almost every instance, these men of God contributed to my success. They provided words of encouragement, advice, and counsel on how to navigate and manage success. I did not have a lot of close friends; I kept things close to the chest because I didn't want to put myself in a position where other people could measure and determine how successful I was in their eyes.

> **"Be nice to the people you meet on your way up the ladder because you'll meet them on your way down."**

I kept my focus on working hard, and I now advise my mentees that they should do the same. I also remind them to "be nice to the people you meet on your way up the ladder because you'll meet them on your way down."[64] It is so important to be honest and fair in the places you are at and with the people you have around you. There are hidden treasures among your friends and business associates. The Lord has ordered my steps to live in several places and to cross paths with many people, *"for such a time as this."* Look at God!

TRUSTED ADVISORS
SUCCESSION PLANNING
RELATIONSHIPS CAN'T BE TRANSFERRED—
RELATIONSHIPS HAVE TO BE EARNED

As I mentor my employees, I remind them that the one thing you can't transfer is relationships. As you think on succession planning, it is important for your replacements to become engaged with the people you do business with. It is important for them also to connect with their peers in various organizations you do business with. Mentoring fosters relationship building, and it costs the mentor nothing. An old adage from Thomas Jefferson is: "A candle loses nothing when it lights another candle."

In any organization, an important strategy is one where participants develop relationships that can keep businesses working with each other. It is just as important to know the "gatekeepers" like the secretary's names, or the engineers, as it is to know the CEO's name. I tell my employees that they should remember, however, that the big shot, the president of a company, puts his pants on one leg at a time just like they do! Everyone in a company is valuable in their assigned role.

SUPPORTING POLITICAL LEADERS
"The Prayers of the Righteous Avail Much" (James 5:16).

The most successful politicians understand that leadership is an action, not a position. I support and pray for our political leaders, as scripture instructs. For the Bible tells us to give THANKS for the leaders that the LORD has given us. We, the people of the community, BIND the will of each politician to GOD's will, their minds to the mind of Christ, and their emotions to the control of the Holy Spirit.

I pray that their every attitude be an expression of the fruit of the spirit … love, joy, peace, patience, goodness, faithfulness, gentleness, and self-control. I pray for the deliverance and salvation of our leaders, our kindred, and our acquaintances who are following the course and fashion of this crooked and perverse world. I pray the Lord will loose them!

I consider myself to be a good citizen. I VOTE, but I understand that it is NOT man who picks his leaders. GOD raises up leaders and orchestrates the events that raises them to POWER. I ask the LORD to forgive us for needless complaining and criticizing. In times of solitude, I pray about local and global politics; that small, still voice reminds me that the power of office or position belongs to GOD and GOD alone. I pray for and ask God to stir up leaders to every good work and good word. I want political leaders who can give cities and states a receptivity to spiritual and cultural reform. They should focus on healing fractures of race, wealth, and ego. We want a community of charity and compassion to create that city on a hill—a beacon!

CHAPTER 15

A LEADER'S
OBLIGATION AND DUTY

CONTRIBUTE TO THE
GREATER GOOD

*Greater good: the benefit of the public,
of more people than oneself*

I had it ingrained in me that I was contributing to the greater good of the organizations that I worked for and with. I felt that I had a duty to help. I work with the organizations that I serve to break down the walls that separate people from one another ... socially, politically, economically, racially and by gender. I want the groups and the families who I work with and around to have more opportunities than I did and to be successful with their goals. When the organizations I worked for reached their goals and we could see our efforts and our goals achieved, only then did I see us as successful. As a leader, I claimed success when my organization accomplished what we set out to do. It was even more rewarding when the original goal was not always clearly defined, but at the end of the day, it was a benefit to others, and it was here that I found joy. We were contributing to the greater good.

I have been blessed to have served on boards and organizations with important folks and many who are the modern-day equivalent of the KINGS of our CULTURE. Access to nationwide networks has enhanced my ability to contribute to individual or group efforts that address the local, state, or national greater good. I believe that each of us has a gift … a talent … a means … a heart … to contribute to the GREATER GOOD of our local and global community. There are times when our goodness is taken for granted. I've gently and compassionately found ways to remind benefactors of neighborhood assistance, that they are recipients of the kindness of the purveyors of good will. It is intended to be a helping hand—not a handout. My Dad and grandfather regularly reminded us that "There is no such thing as a free lunch—somebody paid for it." Sometimes I am approached by those who appear to be unmotivated or lazy folks asking for a helping hand. Although I can't determine what is in a person's heart, I confess that more than once I had the urge to tell them that a helping hand can always be found attached to their arm!

Working for the greater good means that instead of focusing all our actions and time on our own advancement, we should also be focusing on how our actions will improve the greatest number. The greatest leaders and influencers that we know have contributed in some way to the betterment of how humans think, act, feel, and behave. They have improved or elevated us in some way or another and, more importantly, they have changed what we thought was possible. I pray that the Lord will give each of us a place and portion amongst such godly men and women.

Neither the Christian community, the civic leaders, nor government officials can remain silent about vital moral and religious issues. Government cannot be neutral toward religion. Secularism is a religion. Neutrality is a myth. It is as true today as it was in the 17th century when Irish statesman Edmund Burke said, "The only thing necessary for the triumph of evil is for good men to do nothing." We only realize the importance of our voices when we are silenced. Let us hope that we as a populace don't wait until then.

As a business leader, I understand that contributing to the "Greater Good" extends far beyond the walls of my company or the boardrooms of organizations that I serve on. Formally and informally, I've dealt with the following "Greater Good" responsibilities:

- Things that are greater than ourselves.
- Things that benefit others.
- Things that contribute to the well-being of society.
- Things that represent standards of well-being for all of us.
- Things that support justice and peace.
- Things that develop healthy social systems.

Also, in the delivery of GREATER GOOD goals, leaders should remember to be respectful to those they are serving, to consider diverse and inclusive goals, and to act as citizens of the global community.

Discussions about the Greater Good is no new phenomena. Philosophically, in modern times, practical politics and political correctness means ignoring facts. Ancient philosophers took positions concerning the "Greater Good" of society. Socrates believed that his mission was to examine his fellow citizens and persuade them that the most important good for a human being was the health of the soul. Wealth, he insisted, does not bring about human excellence or virtue, but virtue makes wealth and everything else good for human beings. From another perspective, ancient philosopher Aristotle's search for the Greater Good was a search for the highest good, and he assumes that the highest good, whatever it turns out to be, has three characteristics: it is desirable for itself, it is not desirable for the sake of some other good, and all other goods are desirable for its sake.

Aristotle further defined contributors to the Greater Good as those who achieve a well-lived life. He states that this goal is engaged in, pursued, or, quite simply, done. On this account, a well-lived life is, as it were, both the race and the medal won. Current followings and study of the Greater Good concept can be found in academic, political, and social circles. For instance, Berkley University has a Greater Good Science Center that develops science-based practice for building kinder, happier schools; the University of Texas studies the ethics term for Greater Good simply as utilitarianism; and Stanford University defines utilitarianism from a historical perspective in their Encyclopedia of Philosophy. In my life, the acceptance of the Greater Good aligns with the Socratic definition.

Generational Wealth – Passing It On Succession Plans

One generation plants a tree, and the next generation gets the shade. (Chinese Proverb)

It is well known that there is a widespread generational wealth gap between Black and White populations. Since the 1865 Emancipation Proclamation, Black families have made great strides in improving their level of financial security. A good percentage have achieved financial independence through participation in trade and industry as well as entrepreneurial ventures. However, there is still a significant wealth gap, as reported by credible organizations like the Pew Research Center, the Urban Institute, and the Federal Reserve Bank. There is an even wider disparity relative for Black families passing wealth from one generation to the other. Financial advisors and academics define generational wealth as financial assets that are passed down through families to children, grandchildren, and beyond. Assets passed from one generation to the next might include cash, stocks, bonds, investments, and property. Generational wealth can also be created through inheritance and life insurance policies. A good analogy for passing on wealth to the next generation is in a popular Chinese proverb: "The best time to plant a shade tree was 20 years ago. The second-best time is now!"

When Black businessmen in my father's generation started to retire, they either had to close the business or put it on the shelf due to lack of succession planning. In most cases, there was no one to pick up where they left off. About ten years ago, those of us in the Minority Business community who had businesses with some degree of wealth began to talk about succession planning. In most cases, the wealth was a result of years of hard work, careful management of resources, and accumulation of assets. Even if that wealth is in the form of fame, fortune, or reputation, it is worth something. It is worth preserving. My "baby boomer" generation of small-business owners have significant worth and growth potential in their businesses. The saying that "you can't take it with you" is an absolute truth. Rich folks need to be reminded that there has never been a funeral hearse with a trailer full of loot headed to a funeral with a body and the spoils of life. One should remember that no matter how big your house is, how recent your car is, or how big your bank account is, our graves will be the same size—it behooves us to stay humble!

> **"No matter how big your house is, how recent your car is, or how big your bank account is, our graves will be the same size—it behooves us to stay humble!"**

Summary of Thoughts on Success and Leadership

It's not due to luck; it's due to hard work.

Hard work leads to success. Some people succeed because they have advantages that make it easy for them. Most succeed, however, because they are determined to. From time to time, competitors or haters say that I am just lucky. I respond to them by saying

> **"I think that society considers too much the good luck of the early bird and not enough the bad luck of the early worm."**

that "the harder I work, the luckier I get." For those who believe in luck, consider what President Franklin Delano Roosevelt said: "I think that society considers too much the good luck of the early bird and not enough the bad luck of the early worm." Luck assumes that success or failure is brought about by chance rather than through one's actions. I do not believe in luck. Luck is based on superstition. I am an optimist. My mindset creates self-fulfilling prophesies by pushing forward and expecting the best outcome. I accept and give testimony that I am not lucky, I'm blessed. Undeterred by minor or sometimes major setbacks, the so called "lucky" person who perseveres has a greater chance of producing a positive outcome. I have figured out that many big shots are only little shots who kept shooting.

My definition of good leadership is being able to leverage the talent of a group of employees to create results, adapt to change, and make a difference. I believe if a person or a group really wants to get something done, they will find a way to do it. If not, they will find an excuse. During my Dad's generation, they got advice like, "If you'd spend more time sharpening the ax, you'd spend less time chopping wood."[65] The Bible addresses the concept of LUCK in scripture as a form of idolatry.

> **"If you'd spend more time sharpening the ax, you'd spend less time chopping wood."**

The first thing I am most proud of is my contribution to civic and social causes, i.e., paying my civic rent. Paying your civic rent describes the act of repaying the community for what it has done for you. I pay back for the privileges I have been given. The road to success can be long and stressful, and most folks could use guidance and encouragement. It is my intent that QUOTES used in my leadership stories plus the list of QUOTES at the end of the sections are empowering, enlightening, and energizing. They can keep you encouraged as you endure the hardships of life and business.

The second most important thing is my public profession of faith through Marketplace Ministry. I'm not ashamed of my faith. I will take the time to sit down with an employee and pray with them. Living my faith in the day-to-day operation of my business has not only been a blessing to me but to my employees and their families as well. My leadership journey allows me to address my daily prayer request: "Lord, out of my life let Jesus shine; make me a blessing to someone today."

ADAGES FROM MY LEADERS

- LEADERS: We want political leaders to foster a government OF the people, BY the people and FOR the people.

- We pray that our leaders will use their power to suppress VICE and support VIRTUE.

- We ask our leaders to BAPTIZE their every thought in the Word of GOD and that you prayerfully seek the mind of Christ.

- We pray that skillful and godly wisdom abides in your hearts.

- Give us a community where virtuous men and women are protected and preserved.

- After all is said and done, most of the time more is said than done. (Aesop)

- A barking dog is more useful than a sleeping lion. (Washington Irving)

- You can take the day off, but you can't take it back.

- You don't have to be sick to get better. (Michael Josephson)

- Everything is funny as long as it happens to someone else. (Will Rogers)

- To lead the orchestra, you must be willing to turn your back to the crowd. (Multiple sources)

- If you are the smartest one in your group of friends … get some smarter friends. (Steve Harvey)

- If you have to tell folks how important you are, it means that you are not. (Greg Lambert)

- I often run into folks who validate my inherent distrust for strangers.

- People ask the difference between a leader and a boss, the leader leads, and the boss drives. (Theodore Roosevelt, 26th president of the US)

- It has been my experience that mingling with wise folks makes you wiser. (Proverbs 9:9)

- Shame on you if you make a fool of me once; shame on me if you make a fool of me twice. (Anthony Weldon)

- No great advantage has ever been made in science, religion, or politics without controversy. (Otto Von Bismarck)

- The first time a mule kicks you, it is the mule's fault; the second time that the mule kicks you, it is your fault. (Mark Twain)

- I start with the premise that the function of leadership is to produce more leaders, not more followers. (Ralph Nader)

- *A good leader takes a little more than his share of the blame and a little less than his share of the credit. (Arnold Glasgow)

- Keep your fears to yourself but share your courage with others. (Robert Louis Stevenson)

- Throughout the history of world governments, we see that the PENALTY good men pay for indifference to public affairs is to be ruled by EVIL men. (Plato)

SECTION 3

MY LORD

SPECIAL ACKNOWLEDGEMENT

Pastor deTreville F. Bowers, Jr. is a friend, confidant, and spiritual advisor to Dr. Louis Lynn. The origin of their relationship is based on their paths crossing during their Spiritual Walk. Pastor Bowers earned a law degree from University of South Carolina prior to attending seminary at Columbia Bible College, now Columbia International University. Dr. Lynn earned a PhD and worked in the agrichemical industry for over 25 years prior to attending Columbia International University. Both men attended seminary at Columbia International University during different time periods. Their paths crossed when Dr. Lynn often attended Sunday afternoon services at Pastor Bowers' church in Columbia—Christ Church of the Carolinas.

Dr. Lynn also attended weekly Bible Studies with Pastor Bowers at a downtown Columbia Bank. Pastor Bowers is a Bible Scholar and a prolific writer. Many of Dr. Lynn's beliefs and Bible scholarship are based on the teaching and preaching of Pastor Bowers, especially in one of his published devotionals titled *Godspeed*. Pastor Bowers encouraged Dr. Lynn in the writing of this section of the book, and he is aware that he significantly influenced this part of the book: Section 3, My Lord.

CHAPTER 16

My Religious Foundation

*"Before I formed you in the womb, I knew you,
before you were born, I set you apart" (Jeremiah 1:5).*

The church that I attended in Lydia, South Carolina, as a child anchored my belief system in alignment with the beliefs of my parents and my ancestors. The foundation of my religious beliefs is tied to my ancestral church, Ebenezer United Methodist Church. The history of that church dates back to the time when my ancestors were slaves. Many of the policies and practices of that rural church came from prior generations of slaves and newly freedmen.

I can trace my family back to the days of slavery in the South. They were brought in from West Africa to the slave trade blocks in Charleston, South Carolina, and became farm workers.

During a 2014 business trip to Ghana, Africa, I told my government host that a lot of his people reminded me of people that I knew in South Carolina. In his royal posture, he replied, "Son, these are your ancestors … your bloodline comes from the trade ships of Accra to Charleston." It turns out that Angola and Ghana, previously known as the Gold Coast, accounted for over 50% of the slave trade to Charleston.

During centuries of slavery, the slaves tried to maintain the religious practices of their homeland. At the turn of the 18th century, most slaves in the U.S. had not been converted to Christianity. However, that changed during the mid-1800s, when there was a huge influx of evangelism as a result of revivals and camp meetings. Many slave owners and overseers encouraged the slaves to practice Christianity under the preaching of slave preachers. Slave family names were often changed, with slaves taking on the names of their owners. After the Emancipation Proclamation on March 21, 1865, the government promised former slaves 40 acres and a mule, but that grant was reversed. After the land grant was reversed, many former slaves decided to become wage workers or sharecroppers with their former owners. Many former slave families also took on the last names of their former owners. In addition to working the land, they also took on the religious beliefs and practices of their landowners even though they did not worship together.

There were very few racially integrated churches in the South other than those that were sponsored by slave owners. There were not many formally educated and trained Black preachers. Eventually, in the late 1800s, Black church denominations, especially the AME, Baptist, and Methodist, established colleges to train educators, lawyers, and clergy. These seminaries include Howard University, Morehouse College, Allen University, Benedict Institute, Spellman College, Virginia Union, and Wilberforce University. My grandmother Salama Lynn attended an AME-supported college, Allen University in South Carolina, to become a teacher.

Many successful preachers used their K-12 education as a platform to intern under already accomplished preachers. Accomplished preachers were considered to be men who had already received denominational credentials to preach. This was not a formal training, or even ceremonial, for these itinerant preachers were ordained by God when they accepted the call to the ministry.

These "called out" pastors were typically assigned by bishops as the pastor for several churches in the same geographical area; they were called a Charge. The preachers received a salary from their congregations and from the denominational bishops. Early post-slavery churches also provided housing for preachers, called parsonages. Most churches in the Black community held services in primitive buildings. These churches were modeled after the White churches, but the aesthetics weren't as good. Black preachers were highly respected and were often leaders in community affairs.

Due to most families being tied to the farms where they came from, when it was time for the children to marry, it was customary to seek out mates in the same geographic area. In addition, social proximity influenced what seemed like arranged marriages. This proximity was based on church attendance and/or business relationships. The union of my parents can be described as Clarence Lynn's (Ebenezer Methodist Church) oldest boy Lawton marrying BJ Evans' (Sandy Grove Methodist Church) oldest daughter, Dorothy. Even though my wife Audrey's family attended a different local church from my family, the community felt that that Audrey and I were going to get married. A similar storyline resulted: Lawton Lynn's (Ebenezer Methodist Church) son Louis married Robert Johnson's (Shiloh United Methodist Church) oldest daughter, Audrey. These churches are all within 15 miles of one another. In some instances, the same circuit preacher was assigned to two or more of these churches.

> **"One of my favorite traditions at my ancestral church was the Fifth Sunday dinner, when each family brought a dish, and everyone "broke bread" together."**

One of my favorite traditions at my ancestral church was the Fifth Sunday dinner, when each family brought a dish, and everyone "broke bread" together. We kids knew which church mother had the best desserts! I also learned and participated in many holiday church events, like Christmas programs and Easter programs. In addition, I either served at or attended weddings, funeral services, and other special occasions. There were church organizations with annual days, where all were expected to participate. During my adolescent years, the church also served as the headquarters for those active in the Civil Rights Movement to

156

pray and inform members and others from the nearby community about marches and other demonstrations. The song "We Shall Overcome" turned out to be appropriate from both the spiritual and activist viewpoint.

Church members took their places and positions in the church seriously. In many instances, talented members who were underemployed in menial day jobs were the deacons and business leaders of the church. Members were faithful about coming to mid-week services to pray, to have fellowship, and to galvanize their strength to fight for the issues facing the community. They became increasingly more important as a meeting place during the early days of the Civil Rights Movement. Whatever the purpose of the event, people came together to worship God, work for the betterment of the community, or maybe just to socialize over a good Sunday meal.

CHAPTER 17

MY CHILDHOOD YEARS

WHERE I BEGAN MY SPIRITUAL JOURNEY

You can't have a physical transformation until you have a spiritual transformation.[66]

I was raised in a Christian home where, as I stated previously, Daddy was boss, and Jesus was King; I also had the benefit of a praying Mama. As a child, I was raised in an atmosphere where Sunday was a revered day. We respected the Sabbath, and we lived by biblical principles. No one was afraid during my growing up years to acknowledge the Ten Commandments. People even had posters on the walls showing the Ten Commandments. I saw my parents and my grandparents live by The Ten Commandments, so I knew it was possible for me to do also. We kids even had clothes we only wore to church that we called our Sunday clothes. I don't remember missing too many Sundays of going to the local country church where my Daddy and his family, my uncles and my grandfathers, had grown up.

As a child, I didn't realize how many folks were pouring into my physical and spiritual well-being. These folks included teachers, coaches, preachers, and community leaders—some of whom became my mentors. I can't discount the wisdom that was poured out by the deacons and mothers of the church. I know now that many folks prayed for me, guided me, counseled me, lent me a helping hand, and showed me "the way." I wasn't an angel, but those folks were not going to let me become a devil either. The saying that "it takes a village to raise a child"[67] rings so true for me. The folks who poured into me first were my parents, then my grandparents, my extended family, and the business leaders, religious leaders, and civic leaders of my community.

> **"It takes a village to raise a child"**

Submitting to the Lord
Just as I Am
I'm here, Lord, as you are holding tight to my hand.

During my childhood, my religious life included attending Church Sunday School, singing in the children's choir, and participating in church programs. For years, I witnessed people giving their life to the Lord in response to altar calls. I was in awe of the reverence of the altar itself, where bread and wine were consecrated for communion services. Because of what I learned at the Catholic school; altar calls represented an extremely holy moment to me. I was especially moved by the sinners' prayer during the altar call. I knew that the church sermon, choir singing, and worship traditions were a refresher for Christian believers. At the end of church service, I could tell that worship services and communion gave believers the hope and encouragement that they needed to begin each new week.

My mother and other church family moms taught the children proper church behavior during the services. In fact, once the preacher started his sermon, if we got too noisy or got to moving around (wiggling) in our seats, the ladies behind you or beside you would pinch you on the ear and whisper, "You kids stop cutting the fool," or "You kids be quiet." Church and school were the foundation of learning how to behave. They also taught us how to treat people right. In fact, learning how to treat people as well as learning how I wanted to be treated confirmed a biblical concept spoken by Jesus: *"Do unto others as you would have them do unto you"- Matthew 7:12 which is commonly referred to as the Golden Rule.* Sunday School and church behavior was fundamental to me in my social and family life. Old school preachers and teachers influenced me to give my life to the Lord.

I remember that when I was about 12 years old, I often saw people answer the pastor's altar call. I saw people go up and give their life to the Lord and join the church. I can remember as a youngster sitting there thinking and becoming convinced that there was something to this thing called church and giving your life to the Lord. I didn't want to walk up there just to be part of the crowd, so I thought about it seriously. On one Sunday while riding to church, I remember telling Mom and Dad that I was going to join the church and give my life to the Lord. By then, I had mentally placed people into two groups: good people and bad people. For me, the people who had a belief in Christ and who went to church were the good people, and the people who didn't go to church or believe in the Lord were bad people or scoundrels. My parents made sure that I associated with people who had good Christian values and whose moral conduct fit well with our Christian principles.

That Sunday, when the preacher made the altar call, I walked forward, and I remember the choir singing, "Just as I Am." That song still resounds in my heart. I saw that giving my life to the Lord surely wasn't going to hurt me. In my mind, it would put me in the category of good people along with everybody who had influenced my life, whether it was at home, family, church, or school.

When I was a teenager, I was intrigued with Bible stories to the point that, when I was able, I started visiting different churches because I enjoyed listening to the preaching style of different pastors. When I heard a "Word from the Lord," that's just what I heard, a "Word from the Lord." I'd often tell pastors it was as if they were preaching directly to me. During times when I was going through challenges, I could hear that still small voice of the Lord guiding me.

I especially remember the Sunday mornings when preachers gave "fire and brimstone" sermons. Even as a youngster, when they

> **"To me a good sermon is one that leaves me either more committed to my faith walk or more convicted about my faith walk."**

preached those type of messages, I listened. As I heard my elders say about a good sermon, I joked that some of those preachers could "preach the paint off the wall." To me, a good sermon was one that left me either more committed to my faith walk or more convicted about my faith walk, depending on the message.

Those "fire and brimstone" sermons reinforced what the older folks, my parents, and my grandparents told me: "Boy, you better be good, or you're going to hell." The concept of hell kind of scared me. I heard preachers give sermons about heaven and hell, and I liked what I heard. I contend, even today, that if there was more talk about hell in the pulpit, there would be less hell in the pews. True Christians know that the Bible, in the Old and New Testaments combined, promise hell for sinners. Through the Apostle Paul, Jesus told us that the unrighteous cannot enter heaven because of their sins … If you don't go to heaven, the only place left is hell. *"Know ye not that the unrighteous shall not inherit the kingdom of God?"* (1 Corinthians 6:9). On Judgement Day, God will assess penalties in direct proportion to the level of unrighteousness. Throughout my adult life, this belief has provided the boundaries of my behavior and my beliefs.

Various preachers showed me that I was spiritual and that I need only to remember that fact. "The Spirit is within you. God is within you." I began to recognize that the challenges of life will test your faith, and it may seem as if God is nowhere around.

However, God has promised that He will never leave us or forsake us, and as the famous poem "Footprints" tells us, "When we see only one set of footprints, it is because God is carrying us."[68]

By the time I reached my mid-forties, I was feeling sporty about myself. Unfortunately, while climbing the corporate ladder and growing my business, I became more and more of a Sunday morning country club type Christian. I was acting and thinking like "How am I going to get to be old and wise if I haven't ever been YOUNG and CRAZY?" I was drifting away from my Christian upbringing. I thought I could make things happen through my own strength and savvy. Then, one day around the turn of the 20th century, a high-level banker friend and his wife went to a Clemson football game with me in the Trustee Suite. After the game, during a casual conversation, my banker friend asked me if I was a Believer. I was saddened that he couldn't tell. The next week, after the football game, my banker friend volunteered to help me to renew my faith and regain what I'd lost over the years. He DISCIPLED me once a week for 6-8 weeks over breakfasts at a restaurant near his downtown Columbia office. I offer this story as an example of someone being a FISHER of MEN (Matthew 4:19).

As I was going through my weekly discipling meetings with my banker friend, the Spirit of the LORD took hold of me, and I was on fire for the Lord. I totally SURRENDERED to the LORD. I went on a Bible-reading binge and read as many religious magazines or books as I could get my hands on. And eventually, I signed up for the Columbia International University Downtown Seminary classes in their Marketplace Ministry Certificate Program. Our classes were held in a meeting room on the second floor of a downtown Starbucks coffee shop. Ironically, that room was called the Upper Room, which was the name of the room in Mount Zion in Jerusalem where the LAST SUPPER was held (Acts 1:34).

I'm now a sinner saved by grace. Even though I grew up in a Christian home and attended church, I was an unfinished work. "Amazing grace, how sweet the sound, that saved a wretch like me"![69] We are Saved by GRACE. GOD's gift of Grace is without condition. It is not dependent on your worthiness, but upon the character of the grace provider. GRACE is so AMAZING to those of us who have been saved and set free!

From church sermons and from my seminary classes, I discovered that your righteousness is determined by your relationship with Jesus. Unfortunately, it appears that the concept of hell has taken on hard times in America. A Pew Research Center Study in 2021 revealed that seven in ten Americans believe in heaven (71%) and six in ten believe in hell (61%). The doctrine of hell was not a doctrine that was developed by Paul or Peter, or even John. The certainty of hell was clearly established by Jesus Christ. The Lord Jesus Christ spoke about hell twice as much as He did about heaven. There was only one subject that Jesus dealt with more than hell, and that was money.

Church During My College and Young Adult Years

HOW CAN A YOUNG MAN CLEANSE HIS WAYS? (Psalm 119:9-11)

Scripture exhorts readers to walk in the law, for this way of life is the key to happiness and blessedness.

Even during my late teen and young adult days, I was still not aware of the "hedge of protection" that God had surrounded me with. As outlined in Psalm 119, walking the straight path of obedience to God's law requires a straight heart even as it creates such a heart. The psalms proclaims that God's word guides and sustains all those who attend to it carefully. At that time of my life, I was also not cognizant of the influence of the church on my life, that in fact the church was a hedge of protection around me. I didn't realize until later in life that churches had been the common denominator of benefits in my life, they were my home away from home. Until recently, the people that I attended church with looked just like me. During my childhood, it was obvious that in South Carolina, Sunday (church day) was the most segregated day of the week. Until the 1990s, there were few churches that had integrated congregations. There were Black churches and White churches in most small towns in South Carolina. Many Southern towns had a prominent Baptist church in their market square that was similarly named—First Baptist of whatever city you were in. We accepted that this was the way it was. I am now a member of a diverse church congregation with an expository-style pastor whose sermons are grounded in the biblical text to provide their theme and structure.

"Since I grew up in a Christian home, I could not walk away from my faith when I went to college."

Since I grew up in a Christian home, I could not walk away from my faith when I went to college. When I first left home to go to college, I missed a few Sundays, but then I started feeling guilty as if Mama was saying, "Boy, get up and go to church." I had a group of friends who had similar beliefs, and we found local churches in this college town we were in. The people at those churches knew we were away from home. They also knew we were the first African Americans at Clemson. Those congregations poured into us, and they helped us maintain a good spiritual foundation. As boys would be boys, we occasionally did what the old folks called straying from the path. When we did, they talked to us. In fact, they would invite us to their businesses or homes to have basement parties. This helped them keep an eye on us and encourage us at the same time. Those church members would also watch over us and make sure we did the right thing. It was the members of those churches who were so influential during that season of my life. Their leadership, their prayers, and their fellowship all contributed to making me the man that I am today.

Part of my spiritual foundation was hearing preachers talk about the fear of the Lord. At some point during my college days, I came to the conclusion that if I did good, the Lord would do me good. Every time I had a bad experience or fell on hard times, I got on my knees and prayed. Praying over my situations was instilled in me as a child. I didn't just say the Lord's Prayer, I prayed for mercy and deliverance in my life. I also prayed for guidance, and I prayed to see my heart changed. I heard my family do that, and I thought that would work for me. You might say, one of my valuable lessons as a child was to learn of the fear of the Lord. I had heard it so much that I knew I needed to have it myself!

How Did I Know God's Spirit Was Leading Me?

One way I knew that God was leading me was by watching how my prayers were being answered; even the prayers that I thought were unanswered. I would see things happen that I had prayed about, and I would hear instructions in my heart. Here's where you often hear me now saying that it's not a coincidence, it's a God-incidence! You hear me say, "look at God!" My answers to prayers are not a result of Aladdin's lamp or from a wish list. They are a result of God's mercy and grace bestowing His goodness in answering my prayers. I've watched my family, my Daddy, my grandparents, my relatives pray at home and at church. When they prayed for specific things, many times those things came to pass. I often heard them testify as to how the Lord had answered their prayers. As I got older and prayed for people and with people, I saw answers to prayer happen to me as well.

In my midlife, I went to seminary to study Marketplace Ministry. Being immersed in the Word of God and having Godly instructors and classmates enriched my life tremendously. My prayer life continued to grow when I found that God would send me someone that I needed to talk with; soon, that person would just walk into my life. As I raised my children, I would pray for them because I wanted them to always make the right choices and be in the right place at the right time. I would pray and ask the Lord for His help and His guidance. Sometimes those prayers were answered in strange ways. I would always know that the Lord heard me, though. When I said that to nonbelievers, they would say, "Oh that's just a coincidence." It was here I would have to tell them, "No, no, friend, that's not just a coincidence, that is a God-incidence!" Over the years I've lived my faith to the extent that folks would say that I was too religious or that I was a Bible-thumper. Socially, I've lost some friends because of this. There have been times when I was talking with friends who would unconsciously start cursing or blaspheming the name of the Lord. When they remembered my declaration as a man of God they would apologize. Sooner or later, I lost some of those friends who were not comfortable being around me.

As I look back on that, I think they may have been spiritually convicted, since most of us grew up in Christian homes and that kind of talk was probably not allowed by their parents. It is never my intent to try to force my faith on anyone; however, I am always trying to do as Jesus told us, to be a Fisher of Men.

"I am always trying to do as Jesus told us, to be a Fisher of Men."

CHAPTER 19

MY FAMILY AND CHURCH LIFE

*The Family That Prays Together Stays
Together (Proverbs 22:6)*

Audrey and I both grew up as members of Methodist churches. After we got married, we chose churches that had a lot of similarity to the churches that we grew up in. The pastor who officiated at our wedding was a Methodist Circuit Pastor who had been the senior pastor at our ancestral home church during different assignments by the bishop. That pastor gave Audrey and I a lot of wise counsel about marriage. I guess it was good advice since our marriage has lasted over 50 years. All our children were baptized in Methodist churches in the cities where we resided.

When we moved to Columbia and I began my business, several pastors influenced me. In Columbia, South Carolina, the pastors of Francis Burn United Methodist Church, First Nazareth Baptist Church, and Christ Church of the Carolinas provided guidance, encouragement, and support during my spiritual walk. A now retired bank executive friend with BB&T, now TRUIST, also helped shape my public expression of faith, which led to my enrollment in the seminary. The Lord put these men into my life, and I am so blessed that our paths crossed.

> "The Lord put these men into my life, and I am so blessed that our paths crossed."

CHAPTER 20

THE LORD BLESS YOU
AND KEEP YOU

*"May God bless you far more abundantly
than all you can ask or think!"*

Over the years, I have grown and matured in my faith. In the first section, I talked about the time of my life when I decided that I wanted to learn more about the Word of God. I was anxious to get more of the Word and to understand more of the Word and to share more of the Word. I was so excited about my faith and my spiritual walk; I encouraged folks to look at opportunities and seek God's guidance concerning them. From experience, I know that opportunity looks a lot bigger passing by than it did coming to you. Thomas Edison said, "Opportunity is missed by most people because it's dressed in overalls and looks like work."

Growing up, my teachers made sure that I didn't lose track of who I was and influenced me not to settle for less than my best. The church would remind me of "Who" I was and "Whose" I was. They reminded me that God was always there to help me along the way. As I've matured, I've noticed that folks want to measure you on your financial clout. Men often measure success against short-term individual goals. Sometimes the difference that individuals make by achieving their goals could seem minute; however, when that personal goal is achieved, it could benefit a large sector of society, which would then qualify as success. Individually, everyone has to define and measure the level of their success and influence by their own terms and standards. No one knows your story like you do. For success is not merely measured by the noted act, it is also measured by how far you have come.

In my family life and in my business life, I can point to people who crossed my path and places where I landed at just the right time for their benefit as well as for mine. As a child, I learned that you should always do the right thing, using the talents or influence that you possess to help others. All my upbringing led to my opinion that church was a necessity in my life. As a middle-aged businessman, because I had to work, I chose to become a part-time seminary student. The program I enrolled in was designed for working adults and was called Marketplace Ministry.

When going through that program of study, I could feel the Lord beginning to use me. One of the prayers I frequently

"Here I am, Lord; send me" (Isaiah 6:8)

pray is the prayer of Isaiah the prophet: *"Here I am, Lord; send me"* (Isaiah 6:8). As I recognize answered prayers and the hand of the Lord in a situation, I always give the Lord glory by saying aloud, "Look at God!"

Another thing I learned at seminary was that my congregation was the streets of Columbia, Atlanta, Denver, Indianapolis, Syracuse, and all the places that the Lord sent Audrey and I via our job relocations. Over the years, in all the places we lived, we tried to maintain friends and social business associates who shared our faith.

I summarized that the Lord put me in places and people's lives …*"And who knows but that you have come to your position for such a time as this"* (Esther 4:14). This is one of my favorite verses. The story of Esther emphasizes the power of God, instructing us to use the blessings given by God to help others.

PUBLIC PROFESSION OF MY FAITH
Marketplace Ministry

My seminary studies afforded me the training to be able to present a Word from the Lord—a word of encouragement to those I meet. Now, as a senior citizen, as measured by societal norms, I accept that my success is greater in the area of influence than affluence. When I combine my perceived and actual affluence with influence, I think I'd say that I'm successful. *Look at God!*

Although my tendency to be outspoken about my faith may be uncomfortable for some, I am not trying to convert them as much as to give honor to my God. I believe that being ashamed of the gospel offends God, and I never want to consciously do that. I also believe that cowardice lacks virtue. I want to honor God in all that I say and do.

As my business grew and my reputation as a man of faith was established in the circles that I traveled in, I saw that I had a platform that allowed me to deliver prayers or a Word from the Lord at public events. The seminary training for Marketplace Ministry also gave me acceptable credentials in secular groups to introduce prayers at meetings or events.

As a Christian businessman, I stayed active in the PUBLIC SQUARE. In fact, participation in public discourse in the marketplace is one of the ways that I PAY MY CIVIC RENT and how I practice MARKETPLACE MINISTRY. Since the 1990s, many government organizations, business clubs, and social organizations have discontinued the inclusion of a sergeant-at-arms and chaplain in their list of officers. I always asked the leadership of organizations where I have served to allow me to either open the meeting or bless the meals with prayer. After doing that for many years, those organizations often just invite me to offer a general prayer or to bless meals. I seek opportunities to STAND in the GAP for biblical morality and holiness, for I know

"Seek opportunities to STAND in the GAP for biblical morality and holiness."

that it is a blessing to be a blessing. In my life, it seems that blessings heighten when I count them.

It was amazing to see that, despite issues of political correctness or separation of religion from government, the Lord has opened many doors for me to offer public prayer. Some of those events have included meals at board meetings, congratulatory prayers, prayers over the death of members, dedication of buildings, and pre-game prayers for football games. After doing this for years, I was invited to be the keynote speaker for the 60th South Carolina Governor's Prayer Breakfast. During that speech, I got to share earned WISDOM and to deliver a WORD from the LORD. You will find many of the nuggets at the end of each section of this book under Adages.

A discussion about my faith is always in write-ups when I receive written civic or business recognition or awards. My work in my business, as well as the reputation I have gained through networking with corporate and nonprofit organizations, has afforded me some notoriety. As such, I have been privileged to be the recipient of many awards. Some of the ones I'm most proud of are the South Carolina Order of the Palmetto (the state's highest civilian award), the South Carolina Legislature recognition; the City of Columbia – Louis Lynn Day presented by the Mayor of Columbia; the South Carolina Icons and Phenom Award: Who's Who in South Carolina Business; The Small Business Administration National Minority Small Business of the Year Award; The National Urban League Quarter Century Club Induction; the 2021 Most Influential South Carolinians; and the Clemson University Distinguished Service Award.

My public profession of faith is not always well received, and sometimes there has been pushback. I accept that those who are attempting to reestablish religious and moral boundaries should expect opposition. It is necessary to be willing to risk reputation and acceptance by weighing anchor and refusing to give in to diversions. In these times, an uncivil war is being waged for the heart and faith of the American citizenry. Our nation and the world have become deceived by ungodly values. The world sometimes adopts a lie and labels it the truth.[70] I PRAY that the LORD will align my life with Psalm 71:18 "*18 Now also when I am old and greyheaded, O God, forsake me not; until I have shewed thy strength unto this generation, and thy power to every one that is to come.* This allows me to fulfill a mission to give to the next generation those things God has taught me.

> **"Now also when I am old and greyheaded, O God, forsake me not; until I have shewed thy strength unto this generation, and thy power to every one that is to come."**

CHAPTER 21

MY BELIEF SYSTEM

PRAISE GOD, FROM WHOM ALL BLESSINGS FLOW

Give us this day our daily bread.

My faith is strictly based on scripture. When we pray, saying, *"Give us this day our daily bread"* (Matthew 6:11), there is no reference to the future. The provision that God allows for us today is only sufficient for today. Many Christians waste present provisions pondering a future that may never occur. I have seen and benefited from those times when the Lord's teachings and commandments have directed my life. So, I often pray, "Lord, order my steps." Jesus hands down a thrilling command: *"Take courage!"* as highlighted in Joshua 1:9. Courage means remaining steadfast amidst difficult circumstances. For me as a Christian, courage is remaining steadfast when others express fear. Courage authenticates faith. Do you ever wonder what God will say about you when you enter Beulah land? If you do with all your might all that which God has established for you to do, surely you will hear your Lord's voice declaring, *"Well done, good and faithful servant ... enter into the joy of your Master"* (Matthew 25:53). Contemporary man is increasingly anxious about his future and often in a state of worry. The Lord says, *"Therefore do not be anxious for tomorrow, for tomorrow will care for itself. Each day has enough trouble of its own"* (Matthew 6:34). In moments of crisis, the wise man builds bridges, and the foolish build dams (African proverb). Man possesses an anxious pulse for tomorrow. Nonetheless, man's fixation upon tomorrow is quite often out of bounds.[71] *"God has made everything appropriate in its time"* (Ecclesiastes 3:10).

> **"Nonetheless, man's fixation upon tomorrow is quite often out of bounds."**

Man's awareness of God's time is unbalanced. Man's focus is generally upon that which has not yet occurred, and this can and often does generate fear. This unnecessary fear is one of the by-products of man's failure to appropriately address the present. We should abstain from all distractions to the work that the Lord has called us to do today (Hebrews 12:1). This is not a veto for the planning of the future, but it does help us to focus on the present (Proverbs 6:6; 1 Timothy 5:8).

Fight the Good Fight of Faith
"If you fight you won't always win. But if you don't fight you will always lose."[72]

As Christians, we are responsible for how we live our lives. Our whole lives have been but a time of preparation for this season of our lives. The remainder of our lives will be measured upon the basis of what we do from now on. A very wise man once told me, "I have been made wise by the errors of my former days, disciplined by sorrows for the many omissions in my life, and tortured by the experience of dwelling among the perishing." I've observed that mankind is swift to trust in worldly armaments and weapons. Nevertheless, as King David said to Goliath, *the Lord does not deliver by sword or by spear; for the battle is the Lord's and He will give you into our hands"* (1 Samuel 17:47). Our dependence upon God is the most effective weapon that we possess.

I challenge readers of this book to think about how many non-recurring anxieties you imported in just the past week. You need to understand that each one of those anxieties pirated from you the strength that the Lord granted you for that day. People who traffic in anxiety are lusting for what God has not provided. God is not going to leave us defenseless. I provide testimony that God will do what He does in the right way and at the right time to bring about the right results.

I try to eliminate and avoid life battles that are not of my own making. I regret and am ashamed of the past battles I participated in that God did not call me to participate in. I know what happens when we are fighting God's battles with our own strength rather than by accessing the power of the Holy Spirit. The non-Christian must fight his own battles, but God fights battles for Christians. Trusting in Christ and obeying His commands assures victory both in this world and in the life to come (John 14:23). Ralph Waldo Emerson said, "Life is a succession of lessons which must be lived to be understood." I have come to know that wise counsel reveals that "experience is the hardest kind of teacher. It gives you the test first and the lesson afterward" (Oscar Wilde).

"Experience is the hardest kind of teacher. It gives you the test first and the lesson afterward"

A LIFE WELL LIVED
THAT THEY MAY SEE YOUR GOOD WORKS
"Let your light shine before others, so that they may see your good works and give glory to your Father who is in heaven" (Matthew 5:16).

By the time I was celebrating birthdays in my late 50s, my wife and I had raised a family, grown a successful business, served on high profile boards, and established a retirement plan. However, it was during my 50s that I questioned whether the lifestyle that I was leading was worth the price that I was paying to lead it. As I look back on the happiest moments of my life, I realize that most of them did not involve money. I remember that during my midlife, when I went to the funerals of old folks who were going home to be with the Lord, I became more cognizant of life and death. It was during this phase of my life that I accepted that we are "living the dash."[73]

At some of the funerals that I attended, the preachers reminded attendees that our lives are made of two dates, your birth date and your death date, which are separated by a dash. The dash is a symbol of the time a person spent living, and it is also a symbol of how the person chose to spend their time on earth. As a message to those attending the funeral, the pastors encouraged us to make the most of the dash. Someday, when the Lord calls me home, I want folks to know how I lived and loved and how I spent my dash. Old age is like everything else. To make a success of it, you've got to start young. Growing old beats the alternative—dying young. I advise other elderly folks not to be afraid of death; be afraid of an unlived life. I advise seniors to live each day as if it were your last ... for someday you will be right. Mae West said, "You only live once, but if you do it right, once is enough." We are all born to die ... the difference is the intensity in which we choose to live.

The wisdom of Abraham Lincoln suggests that "It's not the years that count; it is the life in your years." Many of my baby-boomer peers have observed and now accept that rather than counting the years in your life, a better measure is the quality of the life that you live during your years. In 2015, Country and Western singer Tim McGraw's song "Live Like You were Dying"[74] promoted a lifestyle concept for folks who obviously have more days behind them than days in front of them. The message was to live life to the fullest and do things that you have always wanted to do. Age is the price that we pay for wisdom and maturity. The best thing about aging is that you are not dead. Don't be afraid of death; be afraid of an unlived life. You don't have to live forever; you just have to live.

Discussions about life and death confirm for me that there's something to believing in faith in God. I have seen folks who walked the aisle to "Just As I Am," and as I grew older watching them, I thought that some of them must have lost their way in their faith walk. They answered the altar call to "Just as I Am" and stayed "just as they were," or even regressed. In summary, growing spiritually is for me a way of life. I saw it in many of my family members—my Mom and Dad, my grandparents, and the God-fearing folks around me. It seemed as if I inherited more than learned it. I think it was in my blood. We know that death is sin's traveling companion. Christians know that if you don't kill the sin, it will kill you. You die to your sin, or you will die in your sin. The enemies of Christ and Christians, which are the devil and his minions, are calculating, disciplined, intelligent, organized, motivated, shrewd, well-financed, and sacrificial in their commitment to seducing and crushing Christians. My goal in life and in business is to make the world a better place than it was before I came. To significantly contribute to the Greater Good.

CHAPTER 22

FINISH WELL

"Finish Well; Anyone Can Start Well"[75]

Finish strong ... finish well! God has given all of us duties to perform, and He provides what He prescribes. I've come to realize that when God places a task upon your heart, do it. My policy and my practice are that I do not hesitate or negotiate with GOD. Just do it! For I know that obedience to perform the LORD's assignments assures you of your eternity. Each of us will be held accountable for God's investment in us. However, if we fill our marketplace with words of hope from each other, all the other means of doing good to each other will increase as well.

I often remind business associates of what Benjamin Franklin used to say: "Well done is better than well said."

I challenge you, as does the Lord Jesus Christ, who requires you to make ready a people prepared for the Lord! When Jesus laid hold of you, He changed you. I challenge readers of this book to identify the people that God wants you to prepare for Christ. Search the heart of Christ's spirit for the means He desires for you to capture, then pour yourself out as a drink offering to God in that manner for those particular people. You shall fail to make ready a people prepared for the Lord at the point you determine the personal sacrifice you must make is not worth the Lord, the people, or the effort. Identify and mortify that sin that deters you. These sins include money, wine, pride, and lust.

Throughout life, I have been warned about the sin of omission and commission in my personal and business life. The acts of commission (doing something wrong) and omission (failing to do the right thing) both lead to undesirable outcomes. This theology comes from the book of James 4:17, which teaches *"Anyone, then, who knows the right thing to do and fails to do it, commits sin."* Its opposite is the sin of commission, i.e., a sin resulting from a blatant and deliberate transgression, an action performed.

The elusive quality of life, the most important things in our lives, the things that make our lives good, are not really *things* at all. What is important are the people who make our lives worth living, the people we love, the people we enjoy life with, and the people we care for. I work at finding balance in my life so that I can devote my life to doing good, to bringing sanctity

"For I know that when we help others enjoy the blessings of a good life, we come to fully realize and enjoy the blessings in our own lives."

into my life and into the lives of others, and to fighting for justice and defending the weak. For I know that when we help others enjoy the blessings of a good life, we come to fully realize and enjoy the blessings in our own lives.

I am old enough to see some disturbing social changes both in individuals and in the overall world order. Today's world has taken away so many things that this country boy grew up with. It has taken the melody out of music, the pride out of appearance, the refinement out of language, the courtesy out of driving, the commitment out of marriage, the responsibility out of parenthood, the civility out of behavior, the Golden Rule from rulers, and it has even taken God out of government and school.

As Pastor Det Bowers points out in his sermons and devotional book *Godspeed*, our societal boundaries have become blurred. Much of our society is unable or unwilling to distinguish between vice and virtue, between right and wrong. Those commissioned by the Lord Jesus to make a people fit for His coming must be at war with their age. I pray that you never allow your theology or your practice of Christianity to become shaped by the changing values of your culture rather than by the scripture, which reveals a Jesus who is the same yesterday, today, and forever. Your Christianity is tried, proven, historic, and relevant.

We should all work to be one who endures. Those who endure refuse to merely observe surrounding occurrences. If you are saved, then you are a strong warrior to the glory of God. You are an active member of the Lord's army. I believe that each of us will be held accountable for every deed that we did or that we failed to do in this world. Your deeds will SUSTAIN or DEVISTATE your life's Testimony. Each of us should do the work that the Lord has assigned to us, and then pray that we leave a great legacy. I believe that when the ELECT enter heaven, if we do all that GOD has established for us to do, surely, we will hear the Lord's voice declaring, *"Well done, good and faithful servant ... enter into the joy of your Master"* (Matthew 25:23).

> **"I believe that each of us will be held accountable for every deed that we did or that we failed to do in this world."**

ADAGES FROM MY LORD

- Bad company corrupts good morals. (1 Corinthians 15:33)

- Remember that GOD is everywhere—even at your wits end. (Modern adage)

- Know that He will give His Angels charge concerning you to guard you in all your ways. (Psalm 91)

- No great advantage has ever been made in science, religion, or politics without controversy. (Thomas Carlyle)

- The Promised Land is always on the other side of the wilderness. (Havelock Ellis)

- We can complain because rose bushes have thorns, or we can rejoice because thorn bushes have roses. (Abraham Lincoln)

- I never worshipped money and I never worked just for money. I also worked for the Greater Good. (Muhammed Ali)

- If it is common, it is not wisdom, and if it is wisdom, then it is not common. (Francis Bacon)

- Do the Good Works that God has prepared for you to complete. (Ephesians 2:10)

- Fight the good fight. Christ is thy strength and thy right. (2 Timothy 6:12)

- Success is getting what you want. Happiness is wanting what you get. (Dale Carnegie, *How to Stop Worrying and Start Living*)

- Minds are like parachutes—they only work when open. (Thomas Dewar)

- I continually run into and have mastered dealing with oxymorons like resident aliens, good grief, same difference, almost exactly, small crowd, legally drunk, pretty ugly, passive aggression, working holiday. (Public Domain - Various Authors)

- TRUST but VERIFY. (Russian proverb used often by Ronald Reagan when president)

- The achievements of an organization are the results of the combined effort of each individual. (Coach Vince Lombardi)

- The smallest act of kindness is worth more than the greatest intention. Oscar Wilde

- It is better to act and repent than not act and regret. (Nicolo Machiavelli)

- It is easier to get forgiveness than permission. (Rear Admiral Grace Hopper)

- Don't judge each day by the harvest you reap, but by the seeds that you plant. (Robert Louis Stevenson)

THE END

My PRAYER FOR READERS OF THIS BOOK IS:

Almighty and Everlasting, the Creator and Author of all things good … we come together this day to seek Your wisdom, Your guidance, Your courage, and Your strength. We ask you, LORD, to order our steps, our words, our thoughts, and our deeds. We ask for courage and wisdom to be good stewards of the trust and the resources that You've given us. Father GOD … let us discern appropriate advances to protect the "METES and BOUNDS" of society. We pray for INCREASE. Enlarge our territory! We pray for blessings exceedingly, abundantly, beyond all that we can ask or think. Finish Well!

SOLI DEO GLORIA![76]

To God alone be the GLORY

BIBLIOGRAPHY

1. Angelou, M. Harold Bloom, Ed. (1996). *I Know Why the Caged Birds Sing*. New York: Chelsea House Publishers.

2. Tyson, C. & Burford, M.,(2021). *Just As I Am: A Memoir*. First edition. New York: Harper Collins Publishers.

3. Warren, R. (2002). *The Purpose-Driven Life: What on Earth Am I Here For?* Grand Rapids, Michigan: Zondervan.

4. Renshon, S. A. (1996). *High Hopes: Bill Clinton and The Politics of Ambition*. NYU Press. http://www.jstor.org/stable/j.ctt9qg13p

5. John Wooten, in Forbes, *Character Is What You Do When Everyone Is Watching*. October 23, 2012.

6. Character is made by what you stand for; reputation by what you fall for. Alexander Wolcott, critic and author (wonderfulquotes.com).

7. Your character is who you are, and your reputation is who people think you are. *Wooden: A Lifetime of Observations and Reflections On and Off the Court*. McGraw Hill Professional, Apr. 22, 1997.

8. Worry about your character, not your ... The Wizard's wisdom: "Woodenisms," ESPN.com staff, Jun. 4, 2010.

9. Let your character speak louder than your words. Mark Twain

10. It is not how we make mistakes; it's how we correct them. Unknown

11. Public Domain

12. Hans Urs von Balthasar, *Prayer.* Ignatius Press, 1986.

13. While attributed to Ben Franklin, true author is not known.

14. African proverb.

15. https://www.inspireyoursuccess.com/tony-robbins-quotes

16. Malala Yousafzai, July 23, 2013, "Speech at the United Nations."

17. *Puberty is like a caterpillar.* Barre, Robin. https://theshiftlesswanderer.com (blog, Jan. 24, 2023.)

18. *Hard Work.* Robert Half, Businessman, Deep Coaching and the Quotable Coach, 2015

19. Ball of Confusion, That's What the World is Today, lyrics @Sony/ARV Music, Publishing LLC

20. "What's Going On." Songwriters: Marvin Gaye, Renaldo Benson, Alfred Cleveland. Lyrics © Stone Agate Music, Nmg Music, Mgiii Music, Fcg Music, Jobete Music Co Inc.

21. "War." Songwriters Barrett Strong, Norman Whitfield @ Royalty Network, Sony/ATV Music Publishing LLC.

22. Ruth Bader Ginsburg, https://americanwritersmuseum.org/ruthbaderginsburg- ginsburgquotes

23. "Say It Loud, I'm Black and I'm Proud." Songwriters: Alfred James Ellis, James Brown @BMG Rights Management,

Capitol CMG Publishing, Cobalt Publishing LLC, Universal Music Publishing Group, Warner Chappell Music, Inc.

24. Dr. Martin Luther King Jr. at Stanford, 1967, excerpt from "The Other America" delivered in Memorial Auditorium.

25. Mark Twain - made popular on Mash Col Potter.

26. Chinese proverb.

27. Follow the Money: "Follow the money" is a catchphrase popularized by the 1976 docudrama film *All the President's Men*

28. Ethan Greavu

29. James Keller, Goodreads.com.

30. The first widespread use of the term occurred in the March 16, 1963, edition of the Saturday Evening Post, written by George McMillian. The most recognizable internal source of the term is a 2003 Monograph by author Skip Eisiminger that was published by Clemson University.

31. "Just As I Am." Songwriters: Charlotte Elliot, Cyril Loris Neil Holland, Deniece Williams, Loris Holland, William B. Bradbury.

32. Henry David Thoreau

33. Zig Ziglar. *Biscuits, Fleas, and Pump Handles.* 1974. Update.

34. African proverb.

35. Lou Holtz.

36. Peter Drucker.

37. Benjamin Franklin.

38. Malcolm X. (1964). Malcolm X's Speech at the Founding Rally of the Organization of Afro-American Unity.

39. Maxwell, John, Life Quotes from John Maxwell: Insights on Leadership. May 1, 2014.

40. Margaret Thatcher.

41. Albert Mohler.

42. Theodore Roosevelt.

43. Christensen, C. M. (2012). *How Will You Measure Your Life?* HarperCollins.

44. Drucker, P. F. The Practice of Management. *Challenge, Taylor & Francis Journals, 3*, pp. 61-64.

45. Eleanor Roosevelt.

46. *A Short Biography of Eleanor Roosevelt*. Eleanor Roosevelt Papers Project. The George Washington University. https://erpapers.columbian.gwu.edu/short-biography-eleanor-roosevelt

47. Bo Bennett Quotes. (n.d.). BrainyQuote.com. Retrieved May 6, 2024, from https://www.brainyquote.com/quotes/bo_bennett_167552

48. Marie von Ebner-Eschenbach.

49. Dorothy Barnard.

50. Maxwell, J. *Teamwork Makes the Dream Work*. (2002). J. Countryman, Nashville, Tenn.

51. Ruby, J. (2013). *Not Counting Tomorrow: The Unlikely Life of Jeff Ruby*. Ruby and Robert Winder.

52. Welch, J., & Welch, S. (2005). Winning. New York, Harper Business Publisher.

53. John Quincy Adams , Sixth President of the United States.

54. Binder, Texas Bix, *Don't Squat With Your Spurs On!- A Cowboy's Guide to Life.*

55. John Shedd.

56. Alexander the Great.

57. Dr. Kavanagh, from *Moral Anatomy.* Cited in the New Rochelle Pioneer, 1908.

58. Jim Valvano said, "My father gave me the greatest gift anyone could give another person. He believed in me." FB, June 16, 2019.

59. Vernon's Law. Vernon Sanders, American former baseball pitcher.

60. Stephen McGuinness, Southwestern Trading Company, June 16, 2021.

61. Peter Seeger.

62. Plato.

63. African proverb.

64. William Mizner.

65. Proverb (derived from a saying of Abraham Lincoln).

66. Cory Booker.

67. African proverb.

68. Footprints. Unknown.

69. "Amazing Grace" is a Christian hymn published in 1779, written in 1772 by English Anglican clergyman and poet John Newton (1725–1807).

70. Pastor deTreville F. Bowers, Jr., *Godspeed.*

71. Pastor deTreville F. Bowers, Jr., *Godspeed.*

72. Bob Crow. Wind and Fly LTD. AZ quotes.com

73. "The Dash" is a poem by Linda Ellis, written in 1996.

74. Tim McGraw: Songwriters: Craig Michael Wiseman, James Timothy Nichols, Tim Nichols. Live Like You Were Dying lyrics © BMG Rights Management, Warner Chappell Music, Inc.

75. Miles Anthony Smith, Why Leadership Sucks™ Volume 1: Fundamentals of Level 5 Leadership and Servant Leadership.

76. Roman 11:36 - a Latin term from Protestant Reformation Theology

www.ingramcontent.com/pod-product-compliance
Lightning Source LLC
Chambersburg PA
CBHW051515120626
46551CB00012B/935